SUMMER OLYMPICS

THE DEFINITIVE GUIDE TO THE WORLD'S GREATEST SPORTS CELEBRATION

CLIVE GIFFORD

KINGFISHER

BOSTON

KINGFISHER

a Houghton Mifflin Company imprint
222 Berkeley Street
Boston, Massachusetts 02116
www.houghtonmifflinbooks.com

Author: Clive Gifford
Illustrators: Julie Hartigan, Mike Buckley
Managing editor: Russell Mclean
Coordinating editor: Stephanie Pliakas
Deputy art director: Mike Buckley
Senior designer: Malcolm Parchment
Senior production controller: Debbie Otter
DTP coordinator: Sarah Pfitzner
DTP operator: Primrose Burton
Picture researcher: Rachael Swann
Indexer: Betty Lobsters

First published in 2004
1 3 5 7 9 10 8 6 4 2

1TR/0204/TBB/MA(MA)/150LMSLK

LIBRARY OF CONGRESS CATALOGING-IN-PUBLICATION DATA
has been applied for.

Note to readers:
The web site addresses listed in this book are correct at the time of going to print. However,
due to the ever-changing nature of the Internet, web site addresses and content can change. Web
sites can contain links that are unsuitable for children. The publisher cannot be held responsible
for changes in web site addresses or content or for information obtained through third-party
web sites. We strongly advise that Internet searches should be supervised by an adult.

ISBN 0-7534-5693-1

Printed in the Slovak Republic

The publishers would like to thank the following for permission to reproduce their material. Every care has been taken to trace copyright holders. However, if there
have been unintentional omissions or failure to trace copyright holders, we apologize and will, if informed, endeavor to make corrections in any future edition.

Key: b = bottom, c = center, l = left, r = right, t = top, Getty = Getty Images

Front cover: t Empics; tl Empics; cl Empics; bl Empics; c Empics; tr Empics; cr Empics; br Empics; b Empics. Back cover: tl Empics; cl Empics; bl Getty; tr Empics; cr Getty

1 Clive Brunskill/Getty; 2tl Empics; 2tr Empics; 3bl Empics; 4bl Empics; 4tr Getty; 4br Empics; 4–5 main image Brent Bear/Corbis; 4–5c Getty; 5tr Empics; 6cl Musée Municipal
Antoine Vivenel, Compiegne, France/Bridgeman Art Library; 6bl Getty; 6tr Milos Bicanski/Getty; 6bc IOC/Getty; 6br Rykoff Collection/Corbis; 7cl IOC/Getty; 7tr IOC/Getty; 7bl Gray
Mortimore/Getty; 8tl Getty; 8bl Bettman/Corbis; 8–9c Empics; 9tr Empics; 9br IOC/Olympic Museum Collections; 10tl IOC/Olympic Museum Collections; 10cl Empics; 10bl Getty;
10cr Empics; 11tl Popperfoto.com; 11cl IOC/Olympic Museum Collections; 11br Popperfoto.com; 12cl Empics; 12tr Getty; 12–13bc Getty; 13tr Getty; 13cr Getty;
14cr Getty; 14bl Tom Hauck/Getty; 14–15tc Ross Kinnaird/Getty; 15cr Tony Marshall/Empics; 15b Neal Simpson/Empics; 16cl Getty; 16tr Empics; 16bl Getty; 16–17c Getty; 17tr Getty;
17b Getty; 18tl Getty; 18bl Empics/DPA; 18cr Empics/DPA; 19tl Getty; 19cl Tony Marshall/Empics; 19br DPA/DPA (Empics); 20tl IOC/Olympic Museum Collections; 20c Empics; 20cr Empics;
20bl Empics; 21c Empics; 21tl Empics; 21tr Bettman/Corbis; 21br Bettman/Corbis; 22tl Empics; 22bl Getty; 22br Empics; 23tr Empics; 23bl Empics; 23cr Empics; 24–25tc Getty; 24cl
Empics/Alpha; 24br Getty; 25bl Getty; 25br Neal Simpson/Empics; 25tr Getty; 26tl Empics; 26bl Empics; 26tr Getty; 27tr Getty; 27bl Getty; 28tl Getty; 28–29c Clive Brunskill/Getty; 29tr
Empics; 29br Empics; 30cl Getty; 30br Empics; 31bc Empics; 32bl Empics; 32–33tc Getty; 33bl Empics; 33bc Empics; 33b Empics; 34tl Getty; 34bl Empics; 35tr Getty; 35c Empics; 35br
Getty; 36tl Getty; 36cl Empics; 37tr Getty; 38tl Empics; 38bl Empics; 38–39tc Getty; 38c Empics; 39tcl Empics; 39tc Empics; 39tr Empics; 39bc Getty; 40tl Getty; 40c Getty; 40cr Getty;
40bl Empics; 41tl Getty; 41tr Empics; 41cl Popperfoto.com; 41br Empics/DPA; 42tl Mike Hewitt/Getty; 42bl Jed Jacobsohn/Getty; 42c Neal Simpson/Empics; 42–43c Stuart Hannagan/
Getty; 43tr Empics/DPA; 43cr Empics/Alpha; 43b David Cannon/Getty; 44tl Empics; 44cl Getty; 45tr Getty; 45cr Getty; 45bl Getty; 45b Getty; 46 tr Getty; 46cl Neal Simpson/Empics;
46–47bc Empics; 47tl Empics/Scanpix; 47br IOC/Olympic Museum Collections; 47tr Empics; 48tl IOC/Olympic Museum Collections; 48cr Popperfoto.com; 48c Getty; 48bl Empics;
48–49bc Getty; 49tl Empics; 49tr Getty; 49br Getty; 50tl Michael Steele/Empics; 50tr Getty; 51tr Getty; 51cr Getty; 52tr Getty; 52bl Empics; 53tr Empics/Alpha; 53cl
Getty; 53b Getty; 54tr Getty; 54c Phil O'Brien/Empics; 55tr Getty; 55br Empics; 56cl Empics; 56cr Empics; 56bc Empics; 57tl Empics; 57c Empics; 57bl Getty; 57br Getty; 58tl IOC/Olympic
Museum Collections; 58tr Getty; 58cr Empics; 58bl Empics; 59tl Getty; 59cr Getty; 59bl Getty; 59br Getty; 60cl Getty; 60tr Empics/Scanpix; 60–61b Getty; 61tr Getty; 61cr Matthew
Ashton/Empics; 62tr Empics; 62br Getty; 63tl Empics; 63c Empics; 63bc Empics; 63br Getty; 64tr Getty; 64cr Getty; 64bl Getty; 64br Getty; 65tl Empics; 65bl Getty; 66c Empics; 66cr
Empics; 67t Getty; 67cr Empics; 67br Empics; 67bl Getty; 68cr Getty; 68tl Darren McNamara/Getty; 68–69c Adam Pretty/Getty; 69bc Clive Brunskill/Getty; 69tr Getty; 70tl IOC/Olympic
Museum Collections; 70bl Getty; 70br Empics; 70–71c Empics; 71tl Empics; 71br Empics; 72c Tony Duffy/Getty; 72cl Getty; 72–73b Getty; 73tr Rich Clarkson/Time Life Pictures/Getty;
74bl Hulton Archive/Getty; 74cr IOC/Getty; 74tl Hamish Blair/Getty; 75cl Tim DeFrisco/Getty; 75tr Getty; 75br Associated Press

CONTENTS

INTRODUCTION
The Greatest Show on Earth   4
From Ancient to Modern   6
Old and New Events   8

The Great Summer Olympics—Stockholm 1912   10

THE OLYMPIC DREAM
Holding the World's Biggest Event   12
Olympic Dreams   14
Behind the Scenes   16
Olympic Nightmares   18

The Great Summer Olympics—Berlin 1936   20

THE EVENTS—TRACK AND FIELD
Sprints   22
Middle-Distance Running   24
Long-Distance Events   26
Hurdles and Relays   28
Long Jump and Triple Jump   30
High Jump and Pole Vault   32
Hammer and Shot Put   34
Discus and Javelin   36
Multi-Sports Events   38

The Great Summer Olympics—Mexico City 1968   40

THE EVENTS—IN AND ON WATER
Swimming   42
Diving, Water Polo, and Synchronized Swimming   44
Rowing, Sailing, and Canoe/Kayak   46

The Great Summer Olympics—Seoul 1988   48

THE EVENTS—PRECISION, STRENGTH, AND
COMBAT SPORTS
Archery, Shooting, and Fencing   50
Weight lifting, Wrestling, and Boxing   52
Judo and Tae Kwon Do   54
Gymnastics   56

The Great Summer Olympics—Barcelona 1992   58

THE EVENTS—CYCLING, EQUESTRIAN,
BALL, AND RACKET SPORTS
Cycling   60
Equestrian Events   62
Team Ball Sports 1   64
Team Ball Sports 2   66
Racket Sports   68

The Great Summer Olympics—Sydney 2000   70

OLYMPIC ACHIEVEMENTS
Great Rivalries   72
Against the Odds   74
Olympic Facts and Figures/Strange but True   76
Memorable Moments   77

Glossary and web sites   78
Index   80

THE GREATEST SHOW ON EARTH

Every four years on one of the
seven continents thousands of
the planet's top athletes, tens of
thousands of staff, coaches, and
media personnel, and hundreds of
thousands of spectators gather in
one city. Their purpose is simple:
to organize, watch, take part in,
and report on the greatest show on
Earth—the Summer Olympic Games.

The ultimate prize

Designed as a global stage where the best athletes can
perform against each other, the modern Olympics were
founded as a way of promoting world unity and finding
ways for sports to cut across political and cultural
boundaries. From fairly humble beginnings in the
1890s and through crises and world wars, the
Olympic movement has grown and grown. Today,
for many of the world's top athletes, the ultimate
prize they strive for throughout their sporting
career is a coveted Olympic gold medal.

▲ *Doves—a symbol of peace—are released during the opening
ceremony of each Olympics. The Games are intended to promote
friendship and understanding throughout the world.*

▲ *At the opening ceremony of the
Olympic Games the national teams
enter the stadium and parade around
the track in alphabetical order—with
the exception of the team from Greece,
which always leads, and the team of
the host nation, which is always last.*

4

In charge of the Games

The International Olympic Committee (IOC) is the body in charge of the Olympics. Following a lengthy bidding process by a number of cities from around the world the IOC decides where the Olympics will be held (see p. 12). The Summer Games are held once every four years. Since 1924 a separate, smaller Winter Olympics has been staged for sports such as skiing, figure skating, speed skating, and ice hockey. The Summer Games begin with a spectacular opening ceremony in which all of the competitors parade around the stadium in teams under the banners of their national flags. The Olympics are followed eagerly by people all over the world. The official Sydney 2000 web site, for example, attracted a staggering nine billion hits, while global television audiences for many of the events are measured in their hundreds of millions.

▼▶ *Three Latin words—Citius, Altius, Fortius— comprise the Olympic motto, which is engraved on the cauldron that holds the Olympic flame. The words mean "Faster, Higher, Stronger" and were devised by Henri Didon, a friend of the Games' founder, Baron Pierre de Coubertin.*

▲ The main Olympic stadium is the setting for the opening and closing ceremonies. At the end of each Games the Olympic flag is symbolically handed over to the next host city, the Olympic flame is extinguished, and the Games are declared closed by the IOC president.

◀ Olympic merchandise is a big business, with souvenirs, clothing, and toys all for sale. Most of the merchandise features the Games' official mascot. Shown here are the two mascots of the Athens 2004 Games, Phevos and Athena, who are named after two ancient Greek gods.

A global stage

The first modern Olympics, in 1896, were attended by less than 250 athletes from a handful of nations. Today more than 10,000 competitors from around 200 countries flock to each Summer Games. No other world event comes close to exciting and interesting so many people in so many countries. Then again, few international events can match the amazing range of sports on display. In a competition calendar lasting a maximum of 16 days more than 300 different events, in a large range of sports, offer gripping and dramatic action as Olympians strive to be crowned the best. While track and field (with more than 2,000 competitors) and swimming (with around 1,000) are the most popular and well-known Olympic competitions, almost 30 different sports are represented at the Games. The Olympics give less well-known sports, such as archery, wrestling, and weight lifting, invaluable coverage on a global stage.

Threatened but flourishing

Given the prominence of the Olympics today, it is hard to believe that the modern Games have been under threat on several occasions. In the early years poor organization and a lack of interest briefly threatened the Games until the 1912 Stockholm event proved to be a triumph. The two world wars forced the cancellation of three Games, but since that time the biggest threat has come from the refusal of a large number of nations to attend the Olympics in 1976, 1980, and 1984 for political reasons. Known as boycotts, these undermined the status of the Olympics as a truly global event. Yet, since the Seoul Games of 1988, boycotts have been minimal, and the Olympics can be genuinely said to offer the ultimate in global sporting competition.

FROM ANCIENT TO MODERN

For thousands of years people have tested themselves against others with competitions of strength, speed, and skill. The first modern Games at Olympia in ancient Greece were held in 776 B.C. The Games were then held every four years for more than 1,000 years before being banned by a Roman emperor. In the late 1800s, as sports became more and more organized, a movement developed to revive the glory of the ancient Games. This led to the establishment of the modern Summer and Winter Olympics.

▲ *Marathon runners at the 2004 Athens Games will follow an almost identical route to that of Pheidippides, the ancient Greek runner who inspired the event (see p. 27).*

▲ *Ancient Greek athletes performed naked in most events, and women were never admitted to the Olympics, either as competitors or spectators. This piece of pottery, dating back to the 5th century B.C., shows male athletes running a footrace.*

The ancient Olympics

According to ancient records, the first Olympic champion was a young cook named Coroebus, who won the sole event at the 776 B.C. Games, a race over a distance of approximately 209 yd. (192m) called a *stade*. Gradually, more events were included, including the *dialus* (two lengths of the stadium at Olympia—approximately 419 yd./384m), the *dolichus* (24 circuits of the stadium—around 2.9 mi./4.6km), as well as the discus and the javelin. Boxing, wrestling, the long jump, and chariot racing were also added. The ancient Olympics were both a religious festival and a sporting occasion. During the Games truces were declared, battles paused, and no one was allowed to carry weapons. To the winners came a crown of leaves and great local fame.

◄ *Baron Pierre de Coubertin, the founder of the modern Olympic movement, believed in the power of international events to promote harmony between nations. He was awarded the Nobel Peace Prize in 1928.*

The modern Games

In the 1880s a French nobleman, Baron Pierre de Coubertin, came up with the idea of reviving the ancient Olympics as a way of promoting sports and physical activity. In 1894, following years of tireless lobbying, de Coubertin founded the International Olympic Committee (IOC). After originally scheduling the first Games of the modern era to take place in France in 1900, the IOC decided that they should be held four years earlier in Athens, the capital of Greece. Only 14 nations appeared in the 1896 Games, in which winners were awarded a silver medal and a crown of olive branches. The early Olympics failed to capture the world's attention, but they gradually built the momentum that has seen them become the global sporting spectacle that we see today.

▲ *This postcard of the Panathenaic stadium in Athens shows a large crowd attending the first modern Olympic Games. Spiridon Louis (left), a Greek shepherd, won the prestigious marathon competition and was chosen to lead the procession at the Games' closing ceremony.*

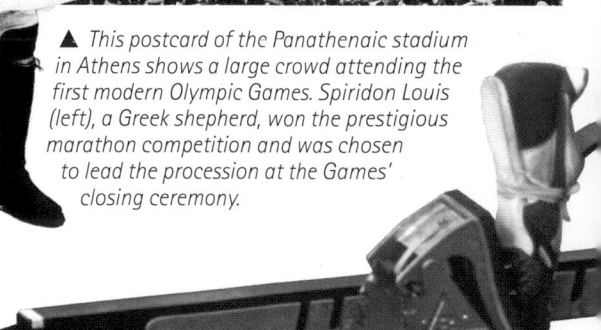

Olympic traditions

Over time the Olympics have developed a strong set of symbols and customs that give the Games their unique identity. In 1913 Pierre de Coubertin unveiled the key Olympic symbol: a set of five interlocking rings, with each ring representing a continent. The following year this symbol, displayed on a white background, became the Olympic flag. The five rings are now one of the most recognized signs on the planet. The origin of the Olympic flame dates back to the ancient Greeks, and since 1928 the flame has burned continuously in the main stadium for the duration of each Games. At the opening ceremony one athlete takes the Olympic oath on behalf of all of the competitors, promising to abide by the events' rules and to display sportsmanship of the highest standard.

◀ *This stainless steel torch was designed for the 1936 Games. It was used during the first-ever torch relay, from Olympia in Greece to Berlin, Germany.*

The Paralympics

Sports for people with disabilities or special needs developed a great deal during the 1900s. After World War II a growing movement to provide an international stage for disabled athletes led to the establishment of Games held at the same time as the Olympics. The Paralympics feature a wide range of events, including track and field, swimming, basketball, fencing, soccer, weight lifting, and judo, all performed within different categories of disabilities. The Games have gone from strength to strength as Paralympic athletes have captured the public imagination with a series of supreme displays of athleticism. In 2000 more than 3,800 Paralympians from 122 nations competed in the Sydney Games. The events were watched live by more than 1.1 million spectators.

▲ *The five rings of the Olympic symbol represent the continents that take part in the Games: Africa, Asia, the Americas, Australasia, and Europe. This poster for the Games of 1948 features the rings alongside an ancient Greek discus thrower.*

◀ *British Paralympian Stuart Braye waits in the "set" position during the 400m competition at the 1992 Paralympic Games in Barcelona. Braye, a sports development worker for disabled people, won a bronze medal in the event, recording a time of 60.92 seconds.*

Time line

776 B.C. First recorded Olympic Games, with just one race

708 B.C. Pentathlon (long jump, discus, sprint, javelin, wrestling) introduced to the Games

A.D. 393 Ancient Olympics abolished by Roman Emperor Theodosius I

1870s Excavation of ancient Olympic site at Olympia, Greece

1887 Pierre de Coubertin has the idea of reviving the Games

1894 International Olympic Committee (IOC) set up in Paris, France

1896 First modern Olympics take place in Athens, Greece

1900 Women take part in a limited number of Olympic events

1904 Gold, silver, and bronze medals awarded for the first time

1908 Some winter events included in the Olympics

1912 First swimming and diving events for women

1913 De Coubertin devises the five-ring Olympic symbol

1916 Berlin Games canceled owing to World War I

1920 Olympic motto and oath appear for the first time

1924 First Winter Olympics held in Chamonix, France

1928 Olympic flame lit for the first time. Women's track-and-field events introduced

1936 The first Olympic torch relay is run

1940 Tokyo Games canceled owing to World War II

1944 Games not held owing to World War II

1960 First official Paralympic Games are held in Rome, Italy

1968 Drug testing begins at the Olympics

1976 First Winter Paralympics

1993 Opening of the Olympic Museum in Switzerland

1994 Winter Olympics moved to take place two years apart from the Summer Games

OLD AND NEW EVENTS

Olympic events are not set in stone. Over the years events have been discontinued or modified, and new ones have been introduced. The number of different sports represented at the Summer Games has multiplied. Competitors at the 1896 Athens Olympics competed in nine different sports. When the Games return to Athens in 2004, 28 different sports will provide a total of 301 different events.

▲ The standing high jump, where no run-up is allowed, appeared in the Olympics from 1900 to 1912. Yet it was nowhere close to being the strangest event—the 1900 Paris Games, for example, featured live pigeon shooting and a 200m obstacle course involving climbing and swimming.

Discontinued sports

Many new sports have been added to the Olympic program, but others have fallen by the wayside. Motorboating appeared in the 1908 Games, for example, while rope climbing first appeared in 1896 and was discontinued in 1932. Some discontinued events, such as cricket (an Olympic sport in 1900), golf (1900 and 1904), and rugby (1900, 1904, 1920, and 1928), are popular international sports. Others, such as the two-handed discus throw and one-handed weight lifting, are rarely practiced today. Many events were discontinued owing to their unpopularity— croquet, for example, was eliminated after only one paying spectator watched the 1900 event.

▼ Tug-of-war was a regular feature of five Olympic Games between 1900 and 1920. Here, Great Britain beats the U.S. in the Antwerp Games of 1920.

Demonstration sports

Since 1912 some sports have been welcomed to the Summer Games as demonstration events. The Olympic stage gives them publicity and a greater chance of becoming a fully fledged event at a later time. Some have appeared in order to allow the host nation to showcase a local sport. Examples include football, which appeared in the 1932 Los Angeles Olympics, and korfball, a popular sport in the Netherlands and Belgium, which was demonstrated in 1920 and 1928. More recently the 1992 Games saw roller hockey showcased in Barcelona.

Getting into the Games

To be considered for the Olympics today a summer sport must not involve motorized action. This excludes motorboating and car racing, among other sports. The sport must also adhere to the Olympic anti-doping code, which fights the illegal use of drugs. The IOC insists that in order for a sport to be included in the Games it must be played in 75 countries on four continents for a men's event or in 40 countries on three continents for a women's event. Despite reaching these targets, a number of popular sports, such as racquetball, karate, and golf, do not appear in the Olympics, while other, less popular sports, such as shooting and Greco-Roman wrestling, do. Some people feel that the Summer Olympics is already so large that events should be removed instead of added—but no major sport or discipline has been dropped from the Games since the 1950s.

▼ Germany's Faissal Ebnoutalib and Jordan's Mohammad Alfararjeh compete in the martial art of tae kwon do in the 2000 Olympics. Tae kwon do first appeared as a demonstration sport in the 1992 Barcelona Games before achieving full medal status in 2000.

▶ The 1996 Atlanta Games saw the popular sport of mountain biking make its Olympic debut. First awarded status as an Olympic sport in 1993, the competition—held over 25–31 mi. (40-50km) for men and 19–25 mi. (30-40km) for women—attracted large crowds at both the Atlanta and the Sydney games.

▲ The Spanish Basque sport of pelota (jai alai) was an official Olympic event only once, in 1900. Since then the game—played in a walled court using a ball and a curved scoop called a cesta—has been a demonstration sport in 1924, 1968 and, as shown here, in the 1992 Barcelona Games.

STOCKHOLM 1912

The official poster of the 1912 Games featured naked athletes as a reference to the purity of the ancient Greek Games. Some nations banned the posters.

▲ The official poster of the 1912 Games featured naked athletes as a reference to the purity of the ancient Greek Games. Some nations banned the posters.

The first four Summer Olympics of the modern era had their successes but were also marred by weak organization, cases of poor judging, and several other controversies. The Olympic movement needed a well-organized, exciting Games, and in 1912 Sweden staged exactly that. More than 2,500 athletes competed in 102 events at a Games that saw the first use of electronic timing equipment. The great success of the Stockholm Olympics enabled the Games to survive an eight-year interruption owing to the outbreak of World War I.

▲ The opening ceremony takes place here in Stockholm's Olympic stadium. Built on land donated by Sweden's King Gustav V, the stadium seated 22,000 people. For the first time at the Olympics a public-address system kept the crowd informed.

Global Games

Although the large majority of the 28 nations were from Europe, the 1912 Games were the first in which competitors came from all five continents. Japan entered the Olympics for the first time, while Australasia (a combined Australia and New Zealand team) appeared for the last time as a unit, winning two gold, two silver, and three bronze medals.

◀ Hannes Kolehmainen crosses the finish line to win the 5,000m. This Finn was the most successful track athlete of the Games, also winning the 10,000m and the individual cross-country competition.

Endurance events

The longest race of any type ever held in a modern Olympics took place in 1912. The cycling road time trial, staged over 198 mi. (320km), was won by Rudolph Lewis of South Africa in ten hours, 42 minutes, and 39 seconds. The final of the light heavyweight Greco-Roman wrestling competition was an equally grueling contest. Over nine extraordinary hours Finland's Ivar Böhling and Sweden's Anders Ahlgren wrestled to a standstill, yet neither was able to qualify for victory. The match was declared a tie, and silver, not gold, medals were awarded to both men.

◀ The modern pentathlon was an Olympic event for the first time in 1912, with the three Swedish entrants, pictured here, winning gold, silver, and bronze. In fifth place was George Patton, who went on to become a famous American general in World War I.

◄ American athlete Jim Thorpe clears the bar in the high jump. Thorpe became the star of the Stockholm Games by winning both the five-event modern pentathlon and the ten-event decathlon.

The world's greatest athlete

Jim Thorpe was a naturally gifted athlete who played a huge range of sports at a high level, including football and lacrosse. In the 1912 Games he won gold medals in the pentathlon and the first-ever Olympic decathlon, breaking the world records in both events. His performance in the decathlon was so good that his score of 8,412 points would have been enough to win a silver medal almost 40 years later, in the 1948 London Games. In 1913, however, Thorpe was ordered to hand back his gold medals after it was discovered that he had played semiprofessional baseball. The medals were finally returned to his family in 1983, 30 years after Thorpe's death.

MEDAL TABLE	G	S	B
U.S.	25	19	19
Sweden	24	24	17
Great Britain	10	15	16
Finland	9	8	9
France	7	4	3
Germany	5	13	7
South Africa	4	2	0
Norway	4	1	4
Hungary	3	2	3
Canada	3	2	3

▲ Solid gold medals were awarded for the last time in 1912. Today gold medals are made of silver with a coating of pure gold.

Swedish influence

Women were admitted into the diving and swimming events for the first time in Stockholm, competing in the 100m freestyle as individuals and in a 4 x 100m freestyle relay. But there were still only five events solely for women, compared to 87 for men. There was a notable outcry when boxing was barred from the Games because it was illegal in Sweden. Freestyle wrestling was also excluded. Although highly successful, the 1912 Games was the last at which the host nation was allowed to exert quite so much influence over the Olympic program.

◄ A men's 100m freestyle race starts in the outdoor pool built especially for the Stockholm Games. The gold medalist in this event was Hawaiian swimmer Duke Kahanamoku, who also won gold in the 1920 Olympics in Antwerp, Belgium.

◄ Ralph Rose of the U.S. lines up a throw in the single-handed shot put event, in which he won a silver medal. Rose also competed in the unusual two-handed shot put, winning gold with a throw of more than 27m.

HOLDING THE WORLD'S BIGGEST EVENT

Hosting the greatest international event in the world is not to be taken lightly. It requires enormous amounts of planning, investment, and commitment. Yet the prestige and publicity it can bring and the chance it gives to regenerate a city or region mean that the competition to host the Summer Games is fierce. The story begins at least eight years before the Games are to be held, when several cities start working on their bid to host the event.

▲ In 2001 Beijing, the capital of China, won the right to host the 2008 Olympics, beating Osaka (Japan), Paris (France), Toronto (Canada), and Istanbul (Turkey).

◄ Jacques Rogge has been president of the IOC since 2001. Rogge represented Belgium as a yachtsman at the 1968, 1972, and 1976 Games.

Bidding to be the best

Any city or region is allowed to bid for the Olympics, but each country is limited to entering one candidate for a given Games. A bidding city has to obtain national approval because staging the Olympics will demand a huge investment and commitment from the whole country. First of all, cities form "bid committees" and prepare detailed presentations. Members of the IOC then visit the sites of each bid to assess the city's suitability for hosting the Games. Many meetings are held behind the scenes as the rival cities try to influence the IOC's decision in their favor. This has sometimes led to allegations of corruption, and the IOC tightened its rules after a small number of its members were found to have taken illegal gifts in the late 1990s. During the assessment process some bids fall by the wayside and do not make the voting short list. A city that receives a majority of the vote (more than 50 percent) wins the right to host the Games. If there is no majority, the bid with the fewest votes is eliminated, and a new vote is taken. Finally, as thousands of people gather in the centers of the remaining cities, the result is revealed. For one nation there is great joy; for the losers, great disappointment.

Planning and organization

Hosting the Olympics is a major challenge. Advances in communication have carried the excitement of the Games to all parts of the globe. This, in turn, has seen a boom in the number of people attending the Games, both as national team members and spectators. A city has to be capable of providing housing, transportation, and many more vital services for the hundreds of thousands of additional visitors it will receive. Major public works are undertaken to improve transportation and other facilities, while delegations from each of the sports that appear in the Olympics inspect the facilities that the host city will offer. The preparations for staging the Games are immense and detailed and include the recruitment and training of thousands of people.

A commercial giant

The first Olympic venue built purposely for the Games was the White City Stadium, constructed for the 1908 London Games for the sum of around $64,000. Modern Olympic sports facilities can cost 1,000 times that amount. Hosting the Summer Games today is estimated to cost more than $1.5 billion, not including expenditure on new transportation links and other city facilities. Many Olympics require help from the government of the country—for the 2004 Athens Games the Greek government is estimated to have financed around 15 percent of the cost of staging the event. Some critics argue that the Games have grown too large and are an enormously expensive luxury that few countries can afford. Those in favor of the Olympics maintain that, if they are carefully organized and promoted, the Games need not be a drain on resources. They can also leave behind state-of-the-art housing, transportation links, and sports and leisure facilities that enrich the lives of local people and future visitors.

▲ The financing needed to host the Olympics comes from many sources. Sponsorship and advertising (pictured) provide a large slice of the money, as does the sale of tickets and merchandise. In addition, the IOC sells the television and other media rights to cover the Games and donates 60 percent of the revenue it receives to the organizing committee of the host nation.

▶ The Olympic Village in Sydney housed athletes and team staff for the duration of the 2000 Games. Afterward it became the suburb of Newington, providing eco-friendly, solar-powered apartments for hundreds of people.

◀ For the 2004 Games the Greek government has spent hundreds of millions of dollars extending its subway system, building a new airport and around 75 mi. (120km) of new roads, and planting more than 250,000 trees. Many new sports facilities have been built, while others have been remodeled. This photograph shows two tennis arenas and the main Olympic stadium (in the distance) under construction in August 2003—exactly one year before the opening of the Athens Games.

Bringing benefits

In recent years the competition to host the Summer Olympics has been fierce—and with good reason. As the world's biggest international event, sports or otherwise, the Olympics offer an unrivaled chance to promote the host city and nation to the rest of the world. While thousands of visitors flock to the Olympics as spectators, many hundreds of thousands more who have watched it on TV choose to visit that city or country in the months and years that follow. Before the 1992 Games, for example, Barcelona was ranked as the 16th-most-popular tourist destination in Europe. A successful Olympics contributed to a tourist boom, and by 1999 the city had become the continent's third-favorite destination. The number of tourists visiting Australia increased greatly after the Sydney Games, and the same result is expected for the cities of Athens and Beijing after their Olympic festivals have taken place.

OLYMPIC DREAMS

Every athlete that attends the Games is an Olympian. This in itself is a great achievement, and for many, simply getting to the Games as part of their national team is the major goal. The desire to succeed at the highest level becomes a dream for many athletes at a young age, and their inspiration may have come from watching the Games or meeting an Olympian as a child. Yet between the dream and the reality lie many years of sacrifice and hard work.

Training

Olympians are blessed with the ability to perform their chosen sports to a high level. Successful athletes need to be physically and mentally strong and have a range of physical attributes such as flexibility and explosive power—particularly important in events such as sprinting and weight lifting—or the ability to repeat an exact movement over and over again with pinpoint accuracy. This is vital in precision events such as archery and shooting. Other sports call for lightning reactions or extreme stamina—the ability to perform at a high level for long periods of time without becoming tired. Raw talent is rarely enough for success, and so almost all Olympians train hard and regularly. For many, training is an almost year-round occupation, with specialized training programs organized by each athlete and his or her coach. Training can take many forms, from improving overall fitness and increasing strength in the gym to boosting leg speed through intensive training exercises.

▲ ▶ *British long-distance runner Paula Radcliffe narrowly missed a medal in the 10,000m at Sydney 2000 but has used that disappointment as a catalyst to win many races since then. Radcliffe trains almost all year-round, running hundreds of miles and spending many hours in the gym.*

▶ *Two months before the Sydney Olympics Michael Johnson injures his left hamstring during the men's 200m at the U.S. Olympic trials in Sacramento, California.*

Making the grade

Only a handful of the athletes who dream of attending the Olympic Games get the chance because a series of qualification plans are used to limit the number of entrants. Selection for individual events in track and field, for example, requires athletes to have attained the Olympic qualifying standard in their events. These standards can be extremely tough, but reaching them may still not guarantee a place in the Olympic team. Nations are allowed to send between one and three athletes to compete in most individual Olympic events, while for the majority of team sports a country is allowed to send only one team. Many countries use national trials in order to decide who they will send to the Games, and shock results can occur. For example, at the 2000 U.S. track-and-field trials Maurice Greene and Michael Johnson—the fastest men in the world at the time in the 100m and 200m respectively—became injured in the 200m. As a result, they could not be selected to represent the U.S. in the 200m at the Sydney Games.

From amateur to professional

The Olympic Games were designed as a competition for amateur athletes who were not paid to perform their chosen sports. For a number of years amateurism was upheld in the Olympics. Professional or semiprofessional athletes—who are paid to play and compete—were barred or, if they entered, stripped of their medals. Over time attitudes have changed. Many of the competitors who took part in Sydney in 2000 were professionals, and professional sports, such as tennis and baseball, have also been admitted to the Games. The best athletes in many Olympic sports now have the chance, through professionalism, of training and playing their sports on a full-time basis. They may also have access to the best training facilities, the best coaches, and top medical staff. However, many Olympians remain amateurs who make enormous sacrifices just to have the chance to compete. These athletes have to train in their spare time, and to reach the Games they must pay their own way or raise money using many different sources.

Winners and losers

For every Olympian who steps onto the podium to receive a gold medal, there are many others who have to face severe disappointment. Being the best in the world as one enters the Games is no guarantee of success. Shock results and inspired performances from lesser-known athletes are a big part of the Olympics' huge appeal. Injury, sickness, or simply not being the best on the day can see the favorites fall. For many athletes, just competing is enough consolation, but for those expected to do well, failure to win a medal hurts very much. Losing is a tough experience, but for most Olympians it fuels their desire to train harder and to perform better in the future.

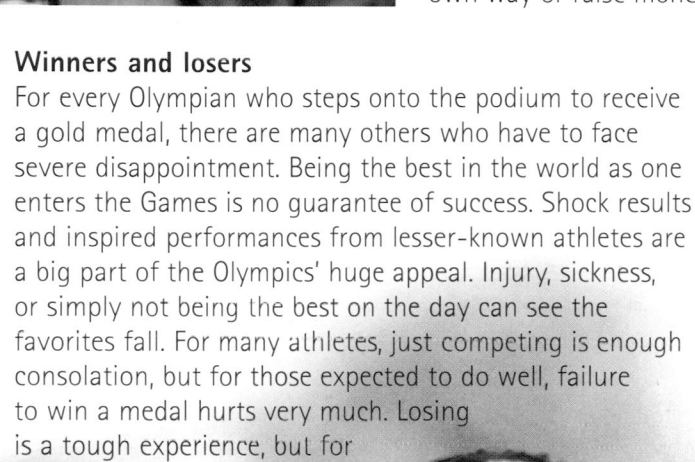

▲ One of the greatest honors for an Olympian is to be the flag bearer for their national team at the opening ceremony.

▼ Nigeria's 4 x 100m relay team is overcome with joy at winning a bronze medal in the 1992 Barcelona Olympics.

15

BEHIND THE SCENES

The Olympics may be all about the 10,000 competitors who thrill spectators around the globe, but without the many other thousands of people at the Games, the Olympics simply could not happen. All types of staff are employed in huge numbers, from experts in information technology and communication, who ensure that results are reported accurately and transmitted swiftly to the media, to the multitude of cleaners who clean up the many millions of disposable cups and other litter left behind by spectators.

▲ Olympic volunteers at the Sydney Games were easy to identify by their colorful uniforms. More than 75,000 people applied for the 47,000 positions available.

◀ A doctor helps Suzy Favor Hamilton of the U.S., who fell shortly before the finish line in the final of the women's 1,500m at the Sydney Games. She had been suffering from dehydration during the race, which was won by Algeria's Nouria Merah-Benida.

Coaches and team staff

A large team sent by an Olympic powerhouse nation, such as the U.S., Russia, Germany, China, or Australia, may contain hundreds of officials, coaches, and medical specialists, as well as technical and support staff. Overall these people stay behind the scenes, organizing the competitors and ensuring that the Olympians and their equipment are in perfect condition for a performance. Many Olympians have a very close relationship with their coaches, who may have advised them throughout their careers. Coaches strive to get the best out of the athletes by devising training programs that ensure the athletes will peak at the right time and by instructing them on all elements of their techniques.

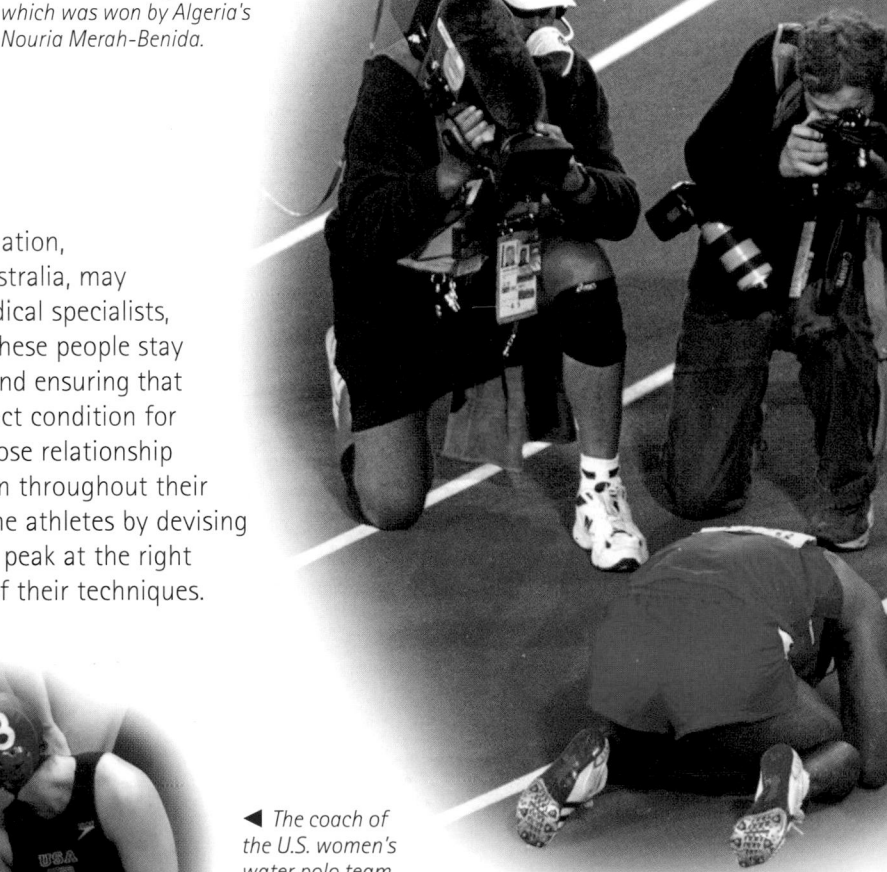

◀ The coach of the U.S. women's water polo team gives instructions to his players during a break in the final in Sydney. His team had to settle for the silver medal after being defeated 4–3 by Australia.

Volunteers

Sydney had 47,000; Athens will have around 60,000. Without them, the Olympics would be chaotic for athletes, officials, and, especially, visitors and spectators. These vital people are volunteers, who give up their free time to assist with the running of the Games. Volunteers are essential, not only to keep down the cost of the Games but, crucially, to give the local community the chance to get involved. Many thousands of volunteers work at the Olympic venues and in the host city itself, guiding and advising athletes, officials, and tourists and acting as interpreters, marshals, drivers, and sports officials. With the arrival of so many people from all over the world, volunteers with foreign-language skills are especially prized. Volunteer positions are advertised several years before the Games, and successful applicants receive extensive training. Their enthusiasm and the warm welcome they offer to foreign visitors is an essential part of the Olympic experience.

▼ *Anier Garcia of Cuba is surrounded by television and newspaper camera operators after his victory in the men's 110m hurdles final in 2000. Media interest in the Olympics is very high, as is expected for the world's biggest event. At the Sydney Games more than 15,000 journalists filmed and reported on the action as it happened. The footage was broadcast to 200 countries— more than at any previous Olympics.*

▶ *Every Olympic event requires a number of officials to ensure that the rules are upheld. Here Great Britain's Linford Christie learns that he has been disqualified from the 100m final at the 1996 Atlanta Games after two false starts.*

The world's biggest hotel

One of the largest projects that a host city has to undertake is the construction of the Olympic Village. In this location the large majority of competitors and team officials live, eat, and socialize for the duration of the Games. Housing and feeding 16,000 people from all continents, religions, and ways of life is a very complex operation. The scale is simply phenomenal. For example, at the Sydney 2000 Games 350 tons of fruits and vegetables, 82 tons of seafood, 100 tons of meat, and three million soft drinks were consumed. These and many other ingredients had to be prepared into hundreds of different meals by a team of around 450 chefs, taking into account the athletes' diets and preferences, and made available to Village dwellers and their guests on a 24-hour-a-day basis. Life in the Olympic Village feels strange for some competitors, but most report positively on their time there. They find that getting to know athletes from other events and countries is a truly memorable experience.

▶ *All types of facilities—from an aromatherapy center to a video games hall—are offered at the Olympic Village to keep the athletes comfortable and occupied during their long stay. This is the Internet center in Sydney, which allowed Olympians and staff to surf the web and exchange e-mails.*

▲ *In 1988 South Korean boxer Byun Jong-Il lost two points for head butting. A brawl began, and Byun was disqualified. In protest, he sat in the ring, refusing to move for the next 67 minutes.*

OLYMPIC NIGHTMARES

Despite its aim to promote peace and harmony, the Olympics have experienced a number of tragic moments. The Games offer an unrivaled opportunity for the world's top athletes to meet, compete, and possibly achieve fame and glory. Occasionally the desire to succeed or the disappointment of defeat has become too much, and competitors have turned to cheating, protests, and even violence. Others have risked their careers and their lives by using illegal drugs to enhance their performance.

Cheating

Trickery, deception, and the fixing of results by competitors have occurred since the earliest Games of the modern era. In 1904, for example, the first man across the line in the marathon, American Fred Lorz, made the extraordinary admission that he had hitched a ride for around 17.5km of the 42km after suffering from cramps. Occasionally the Olympics have been poorly organized or have seen biased judging or major errors in officiating. At the 1968 Games in Mexico City, for example, more than one dozen boxing judges and referees were dismissed for incompetence. One of the most outrageous cases of cheating came in 1976, when Soviet modern pentathlete Boris Onischenko rigged his fencing épée (sword) so that it would register a hit when he pressed a button hidden in his clothing!

▲ *At the 1976 Montreal Games Boris Onischenko has his fencing épée examined by an official after a protest by an opponent, Jim Fox of Great Britain. Onischenko, a former silver medalist in the event, was banned and sent home in disgrace.*

Sore losers

Losing hurts all Olympians. Most take defeat with good grace and sportsmanship, but some competitors choose to protest or take matters into their own hands. This often erupts into spontaneous displays of disapproval such as when British sprinter Linford Christie threw his sneakers into the trash after being disqualified for false starting in the 100m final in Atlanta in 1996. In the men's field hockey final at the 1972 Games Pakistan narrowly lost 1–0 to West Germany. Members of the Pakistan team threw water over the president of the International Hockey Federation and stomped on their silver medals. They were banned from the Olympics for life.

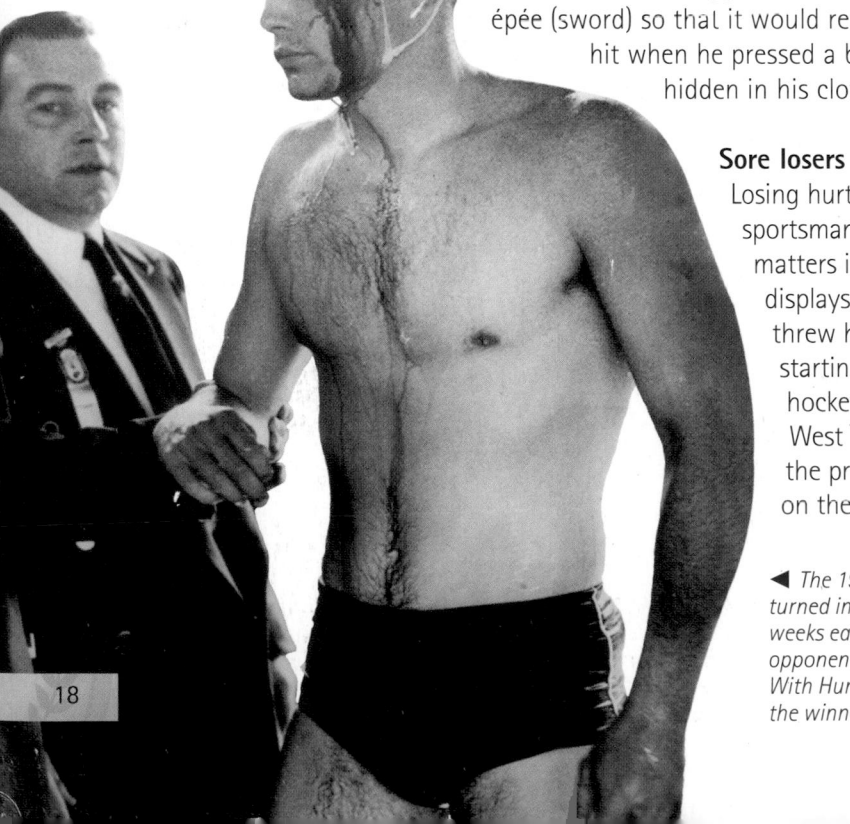

◄ *The 1956 water polo semifinal between Hungary and the Soviet Union turned into a bloodbath. The Soviet Union had invaded Hungary a few weeks earlier, and hostility spilled over into the pool during the game, with opponents fighting each other and, reportedly, causing the water to turn red. With Hungary leading 4–0, the game was abandoned. Hungary was declared the winner, and the players had to be escorted out of the pool area.*

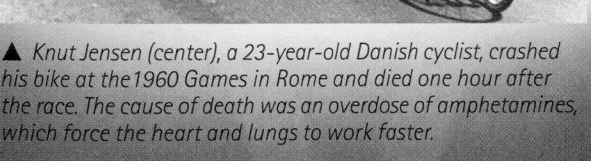

▲ *Knut Jensen (center), a 23-year-old Danish cyclist, crashed his bike at the 1960 Games in Rome and died one hour after the race. The cause of death was an overdose of amphetamines, which force the heart and lungs to work faster.*

Drugs in sports

Doping—the taking of banned or restricted drugs to improve performance—is a major problem in most sports, and the Olympics are no different. There are many different types of banned drugs, including anabolic steroids. These encourage muscle growth, enabling competitors in a wide range of events, from sprinting to swimming, to quickly increase their muscle size and strength. Drugs are banned because they give an unfair advantage to the athletes who take them and also, more seriously, because they are a major health risk. For example, taken over a prolonged period, anabolic steroids can permanently damage the liver, heart, and kidneys, as well as cause depression and uncontrollable aggression, nicknamed "roid rage."

◀ *At the 2000 Olympics three Bulgarians—Sevdalin Minchev (pictured), Ivan Ivanov, and Izabela Dragneva—tested positive for diuretics and lost their medals. Diuretics are banned drugs that make the body remove fluids quickly, reducing an athlete's weight and hiding other drug use.*

Drug testing

The IOC was one of the first major sporting bodies to introduce drug testing. It first appeared, in trial form, at the 1968 Games and was then adopted formally four years later. In the early years athletes found it easy to cheat the system. Today the tests are much more sophisticated, but they are still far from foolproof. Tribunals and even court cases are common after an athlete has tested positive for a banned drug. New drugs are continually being developed, making testing more difficult, but the IOC and other organizations are fighting back. In 1999 the World Anti-Doping Agency (WADA) was formed, and competitors now face life bans for repeated doping offenses. However, the cat-and-mouse game between drug cheats and the authorities is expected to continue for many years to come.

▲ *The greatest tragedy ever to strike the Olympics occurred at the Munich Games in 1972. Eleven members of the Israeli team were taken hostage by the Black September terrorist group from Palestine and were murdered. The Games were immediately suspended, but after a memorial ceremony (pictured) it was decided that they should be resumed in defiance of terrorism.*

BERLIN 1936

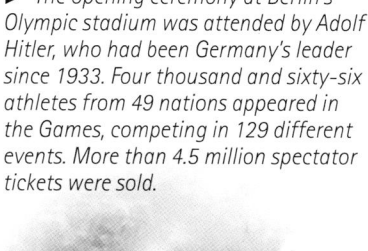

▲ *The official poster of the 1936 Olympics features the Brandenburg Gate, a key landmark in Berlin. The poster was printed in 19 languages.*

Germany was chosen as the location for the 1936 Summer Olympics in 1931, shortly before Adolf Hitler and the National Socialist German Workers' Party (Nazi) came to power. Hitler saw the Games as an opportunity to publicize his belief in the racial superiority of the white German people. Nazi symbols were everywhere; journalists and officials were watched closely by secret police; and Jewish and black athletes were insulted in the media. Yet the facilities in Berlin were the best ever, and the Games saw some astonishing performances.

▶ *The opening ceremony at Berlin's Olympic stadium was attended by Adolf Hitler, who had been Germany's leader since 1933. Four thousand and sixty-six athletes from 49 nations appeared in the Games, competing in 129 different events. More than 4.5 million spectator tickets were sold.*

◀ *Greek runner Konstantin Kondylis makes history as he begins the first Olympic torch relay in the modern Games. Starting in Greece, around 3,000 runners carried the torch 1,900 mi. (3,075km) through seven competing countries before reaching Berlin.*

MEDAL TABLE	G	S	B
Germany	33	26	30
U.S.	24	20	12
Hungary	10	1	5
Italy	8	9	5
Finland	7	6	6
France	7	6	6
Sweden	6	5	9
Japan	6	4	8
Netherlands	6	4	7
Great Britain	4	7	3

Innovative Games

Overshadowed by the anti-Jewish policies of Nazi Germany, it is often forgotten that the Berlin Olympics was extremely well organized. It was marked by many new innovations, including the first modern Olympic torch relay and more accurate timing systems. The Games were the first to be broadcast on television and were shown on a number of closed-circuit screens set up around the city, while newsreels of highlights were flown by airplanes and airships to other European cities. Canoe/kayak, basketball, and handball all made their Olympic debuts in Berlin, while polo made its final appearance. The gymnastics program was expanded and featured two popular German multi-medalists: Konrad Frey, who won three golds, one silver, and two bronzes, and Alfred Schwarzmann, who claimed three gold medals and two bronzes.

Jesse Owens receives the baton in the 4 x 100m relay. He was part of the American team that won gold and broke the world record in a time of 39.8 seconds.

▶ *Owens talks to Luz Long, the German athlete who befriended him at the Games and who was later killed in World War II. Owens once wrote: "You could melt down all the medals and cups I have, and they wouldn't be a plating on the 24-carat friendship I felt for Luz Long."*

One man's Olympics

Few international sports events have been dominated by an athlete in the way that the 1936 Summer Olympics were by African-American athlete Jesse Owens. The son of a poor farmer, Owens had set the track-and-field world on fire the previous year by breaking five world records and matching a sixth in a single afternoon. Despite strong competition in some events, Owens didn't disappoint in Berlin. He became a favorite of the German spectators and destroyed Hitler's idea that the Games would be a showcase for the white "master race." Owens won gold medals in the 100m, 200m, and the 4 x 100m relay. His most difficult test came in the long jump, where he was in danger of being eliminated after two no jumps. His main rival, white German athlete Luz Long, offered valuable advice that helped Owens qualify for the final. Owens then went on to win his fourth gold ahead of Long, who won silver.

Gold records

Jesse Owens's achievements overshadowed many other impressive performances. In the swimming pool Inge Sorensen of Denmark won a bronze medal in the 200m breaststroke. At the age of 12 she became the youngest-ever individual Olympic medalist. The swimming star of the Games was a 17-year-old Dutch girl, Hendrika "Rie" Mastenbroek, who won three golds and a silver. Hungary came a surprising third in the medal table, in part owing to their impressive showing in wrestling and fencing, where they were led by Kabos Endre, who won 24 of his 25 contests. Hungary's triumphant water polo team included Oliver Halassy, who played despite having had one leg amputated below the knee.

▲ *Basketball made its Olympic debut in 1936, when it was played outside. Here, the Philippines and Mexico contest a first-round match. The competition was eventually won by the U.S.*

▶ *American diver Marjorie Gestring captured gold in the women's springboard competition at the age of 13 years and 9 months. She remains the youngest individual gold medalist in the history of the Summer Olympics.*

▲ Athletes race out of their blocks during the heats of the men's 100m in Atlanta. To have a chance of becoming an Olympic champion a sprinter must qualify during several heats to become one of eight competitors in the final.

SPRINTS

Sprinters are the fastest men and women on Earth, and the 100m and 200m races are among the most eagerly anticipated contests of the Games. A series of qualification races, or heats, determine which eight athletes will take part in each of the sprint finals. The tension crackles as rivals stretch and focus, get into their starting blocks, and prepare to react to the starter's gun. Years of training are about to culminate in just ten seconds of intense drama in the 100m and around 20 seconds in the 200m.

▼ Before the start of a sprint race the athlete gets into his or her starting blocks and focuses on the track ahead (1). As the signal is given the competitor raises his or her hips (2) in preparation for the starter's gun.

▲ Exploding out of the starting blocks (3), a sprinter drives forward with short, powerful strides (4), accelerating and moving into his or her full running style. A sprinter reaches top speed during the middle of the race. From then on it is a fight to stop fatigue from setting in and to stay relaxed in order to maintain the ideal posture and technique.

OLYMPIC LEGEND

Fanny Blankers-Koen (1918–2004)

Nationality: *Dutch*
Games: *Berlin 1936, London 1948, Helsinki 1952*
Events: *100m, 200m, 4 x 100m relay, 80m hurdles, high jump*
Medals: *four gold*

Fractions of a second

Accurate timekeeping is vital in many Olympic events but none more so than in sprints. Electronic timing equipment is linked to the starter's gun, which sets the clock in motion as it fires. Reacting or moving off the blocks before the gun has fired counts as a false start, and the race has to be restarted. Many sprints have close finishes, and officials are required to judge the result of a photo finish. The 1992 Olympic women's 100m final saw American athlete Gail Devers separated by just one hundredth of a second from the second-place sprinter, Juliet Cuthbert of Jamaica.

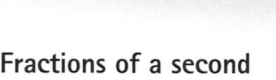

▲ A photo finish is often the only way to judge the winner of a sprint. An athlete finishes when any part of the body except the limbs or head crosses the finish line. Slowing down by just milliseconds can mean the difference between gold, silver, bronze, or no medal at all.

Sprint history

The winner of the first-ever modern Olympic 100m was the American Thomas Burke, who ran the race in 12 seconds in 1896. Over time, with improvements in training, techniques, tracks, footwear, and clothing, times have dropped dramatically. In 1968 American James Hines was the first sub-ten-second gold medalist, recording 9.95 seconds in the 100m in Mexico City. Women took part in sprints and other track-and-field events for the first time in 1928. One of the greatest sprint performances took place in 1948 when Fanny Blankers-Koen silenced critics who said she was too old by winning four gold medals at the age of 30 and becoming the first mother to be an Olympic champion.

The 200m

The 200m begins on the track's bend, with starting blocks staggered so that each athlete runs the same distance. Sprinters power around the bend, and they must stay in their lane or face disqualification. The second half of the race occurs in the homestretch, with the athletes trying to maintain their racing form and style. In the last 20–30 meters sprinters start to decelerate as the fatigue of performing at maximum effort takes it toll. The benefits of hundreds of hours of endurance and strength training allow the best sprinters to minimize deceleration and keep a smooth, relaxed running style straight through the finish line.

▲ Greek sprinter Konstantinos Kenteris cannot hide his delight as he wins the men's 200m final in Sydney. Kenteris followed this success with a gold medal in the World Championships in 2001, and he became European 200m champion the following year.

◄ French 200m star Marie-José Pérec runs the bend in Atlanta, where she won Olympic gold in 1996. Forced to the outside of the lane when taking the bend at full speed, sprinters lean inward to help stay in their lane.

◄ American sprinter Maurice Greene adjusts his race number before going on to win the 100m gold medal in the 2000 Olympics.

Doubling up

The technique and extreme pace required for the 100m and the 200m are similar, and some gifted athletes double up in the Olympics, hoping to capture the ultimate sprinting prize. In the Sydney Games of 2000 American sprinter Marion Jones managed to do what only a handful of athletes, including Carl Lewis in 1984 and the Soviet Union's Valeriy Borzov in 1972, have ever achieved—winning both the 100m and 200m. Jones added a third gold in the 4 x 400m relay and also won two bronzes. Her medal haul is the largest at a single Olympics by any female competitor in any sport.

MIDDLE-DISTANCE RUNNING

Middle-distance races, run over one or more laps of the track, are some of the most dramatic of all Olympic events. Strength, stamina, and pure speed are important, but a smooth, efficient running technique is even more valuable. Athletes need to move fast enough to stay in contention but with energy in reserve for the final stages, when the pace quickens. Most middle-distance runners have perfected a late burst of extra speed and can sprint the final 100m to 200m of a race.

▶ *Michael Johnson had an unusual upright running style, but he was the dominant 400m and 200m athlete of the 1990s. He became the first man to win the Olympic 400m twice, and he claimed three more golds in the 4 x 400m relay (twice) and the 200m.*

▲ *A crowded field in the women's 800m in Sydney is headed by Mozambique's Maria Mutola, who went on to win the event. Despite being only 27 years old, it was Mutola's fourth Olympics.*

▲ *Disaster strikes during the final of the women's 3,000m in the 1984 Los Angeles Olympics. An accidental clash of legs between barefoot Zola Budd, representing Great Britain, and Mary Decker of the U.S. left the American injured and out of the race. Budd, one of the prerace favorites, came in seventh place.*

Changing lengths

Over the years middle-distance races have undergone changes to their lengths, with the mile replaced by the 1,500m as the blue ribbon middle-distance event and the women's 3,000m dropped in favor of the 5,000m in 1996. The middle-distance events were traditionally dominated by English-speaking countries such as Great Britain, the U.S., and Australia. In 1976 Alberto Juantorena of Cuba became the first runner from a non-English-speaking country to win Olympic gold in either the 400m or 800m. Since then Olympic middle-distance champions have come from all over the world.

► Moroccan runner Said Aouita drives away from a standing start in the 1988 Seoul Olympics. Aouita dominated men's middle-distance running in the 1980s, competing successfully in the 800m and 1,500m and remaining unbeaten in the 5,000m for a decade.

Racing strategies

Top athletes treat the 400m—one lap of the track—as a continuous sprint. They set off from their starting blocks, which are staggered around the bend of the track, and must stay in their lanes for the entire race. In the 800m runners also start from staggered positions. After 100m they can break out of their lanes and head toward the inside lane—the shortest distance around the track. Many 800m races, and all longer events, are run at less than flat-out pace. They are cagey affairs, with runners trying to establish and maintain a good race position before the sprint for medal places begins in the final lap. Runners in the 800m and, in particular, the 1,500m have to be aware at all times of the athletes around them, staying alert to the possibility that one runner or a small group will make a fast break. They must also make sure that as the final charge looms they are not boxed in by other athletes.

Race after race

Olympic middle-distance events involve a series of heats and semifinals before the finals. These rounds of races place great demands on the runners, who must do enough to qualify but cannot afford to exhaust themselves for the finals. Some talented athletes double up in the Olympics, competing in both the 800m and the 1,500m or running the 1,500m and a longer event such as the 5,000m. Doubling up in the 400m and 800m is very rare. Only Alberto Juantorena has successfully competed in these two disciplines at the same Olympics, winning both at the Montreal Games and setting a new world record for the 800m at the same time.

OLYMPIC LEGEND

Alberto Juantorena (born 1950)

Nationality: *Cuban*
Games: *Munich 1972, Montreal 1976, Moscow 1980*
Events: *400m, 800m*
Medals: *two gold*

► Romania's Gabriela Szabo waves her national flag and salutes the crowd following victory in the women's 5,000m in Sydney. Szabo also competed in the 1,500m, where she won a bronze medal behind Algeria's Nouria Merah-Benida and Violeta Szekely of Romania.

LONG-DISTANCE EVENTS

Grueling for the competitors and compelling viewing for spectators, the long-distance events in track and field have a long and illustrious history stretching back to the time of the ancient Olympics. The distances that the athletes run have changed over the years, but they currently range from the 5,000m and 10,000m track events up to the 42.2km marathon. Long-distance events also include racewalking, a demanding and highly technical sport that is conducted over 20km and 50km for men and 20km for women.

◀ Long-distance running and racewalking require epic powers of endurance and stamina. Here Slovakian athlete Peter Tichy collapses into the arms of an official moments after crossing the finish line in the 50km walk at the 1996 Atlanta Games. Tichy went on to compete in Sydney in the same event.

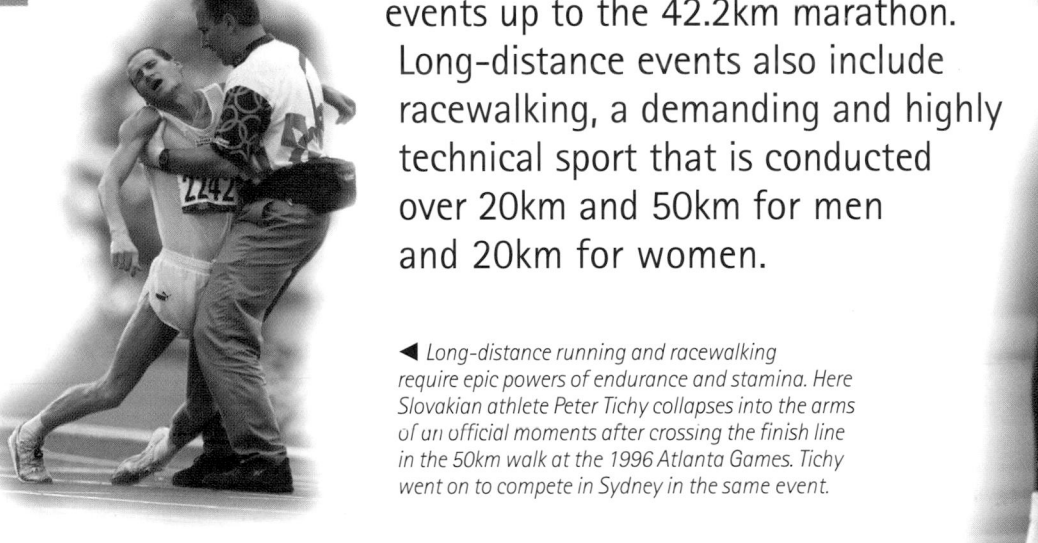

▲ One of the most popular competitors in world track and field, Haile Gebrselassie sharpened his phenomenal speed and stamina as a young child in Ethiopia by running 6 mi. (10km) to and from school every day. As an adult he won gold in the 10,000m in both the Atlanta and Sydney Olympics.

◀ The best long-distance runner of his era, Emil Zatopek of Czechoslovakia set an incredible 20 world records in his career. At the 1952 Olympics in Helsinki he achieved something no other runner has ever done—winning the 5,000m, 10,000m, and marathon gold medals. Amazingly, it was his first marathon.

Long distance on the track

The 5,000m and 10,000m for men and women are the longest Olympic events that are held solely on the track. Racing together in a group, athletes may appear to be running leisurely, but their pace is surprisingly fast and relentless. Competitors in the 10,000m average a little over one minute per lap of the 400m track, 25 times in all. Some 5,000m and 10,000m races can appear uneventful, but fascinating tactics are often at work. Certain athletes choose to lead from the front, while others prefer to stay behind, aware of the leaders but relying on a "kick" in the final laps or an out-and-out sprint finish in the last 100m to 300m in order to propel them to glory. Despite the long distances, races can often end with an extremely tense and exciting finish.

The marathon

The name of this punishing event has ancient origins. In 490 B.C. a Greek soldier named Pheidippides (see p. 6) ran to Athens from the town of Marathon to bring news of a victory in battle over the Persians. To commemorate this feat the first marathon of the modern Olympic era, in 1896, was run between the same two settlements, a distance of just under 25 mi. (40km). At the London Games of 1908 the marathon's length was increased to a little more than 42km. Today's top Olympic marathon runners take less than two hours and 15 minutes to complete this phenomenal distance, pushing their bodies to the absolute limit of exertion. For long periods during the race runners try to maintain a fairly steady pace, yet the key to entering the Olympic stadium in the lead can be knowing when to keep energy in reserve and when to push ahead.

▶ American athlete Joan Benoit waves to the crowd after her victory in the first-ever Olympic marathon for women, held at the 1984 Games in Los Angeles. Although Benoit had won the prestigious Boston Marathon in both 1979 and 1983, Norway's Grete Waitz had started the race as the favorite. In the end Waitz won the silver medal, one minute and 26 seconds behind Benoit.

◀ Racewalking requires athletes to observe two key rules. First of all, they must maintain a straight leading leg, without a bent knee, from the time their front foot hits the ground until the leg passes under the center of their body. Second, one foot must be in contact with the ground at all times.

◀ Robert Korzeniowski celebrates victory in the 50km walk at the 2000 Games. The Polish athlete recorded two unique doubles at Sydney—winning the 50km in two consecutive Olympics and successfully doubling up with victory in the 20km walk.

Racewalking

This event places huge demands on an athlete's endurance and control of his or her body. Champion racewalkers of both sexes can complete a 20km race in only 15 to 25 minutes more than it would take the best runners to cover the same distance. Racewalkers move at an incredible speed, but they must do so while keeping two key rules in mind (see above). Along the length of the course judges monitor the athletes' motion. If either of the rules is clearly broken, a warning paddle is displayed. In Olympic racewalking three warnings result in disqualification. Although racewalkers spend thousands of hours honing their techniques, the pressures of major competitions can cause them to make errors. At the 2000 Games Mexico's Bernardo Segura crossed the finish line believing that he had won the men's 20km event, only to find that he had actually been disqualified in the closing stages of the race.

HURDLES AND RELAYS

Hurdle and relay events call for more than just extreme speed and stamina. They make huge technical demands on athletes, who must execute the clearance of a hurdle or the exchange of a relay baton with split-second timing. In all hurdle races runners aim to clear the barriers with just inches to spare and then get back on the track—where their speed is generated—as quickly as possible.

OLYMPIC LEGEND

Edwin Moses (born 1955)

Nationality: *American*
Games: *Montreal 1976, Los Angeles 1984, Seoul 1988*
Event: *400m hurdles*
Medals: *two gold, one bronze*

Hurdles

One of the most technically demanding of all track-and-field events, the high hurdles are run over 100m for women and 110m for men. Both distances feature ten hurdles, which runners may knock over but with a loss of speed and the risk of a fall as a result. The 400m hurdles also feature ten hurdles, spaced out around one circuit of the track. These are fractionally lower than the men's high hurdles, but the event saps the athletes' stamina as they strive to maintain a regular stride pattern (the number of paces they take between hurdles), along with their fastest running style. Edwin Moses is widely considered to be the best 400m hurdler of the modern era, winning two Olympic golds and staying unbeaten over nine years and 122 races.

◄ *A hurdler moves up and forward off the ground from his or her rear (trailing) leg. The leading leg is thrust over the hurdle, while the trailing leg is pulled up at the knee with the foot turned outward in order to clear the barrier. After the hurdle is cleared the leading leg is brought down onto the track as quickly as possible. The trailing leg is then moved around to the front to make the next stride.*

Relays

The two relay competitions, the 4 x 100m and the 4 x 400m, are very popular with Olympic audiences. They offer a series of sprints with the added drama of the baton changeover, where the receiving athlete starts to sprint just moments before grabbing the baton. In the 4 x 400m the start is greatly staggered, and the first lap is run in lanes. The second-leg runners stay in their lanes as they round the first bend and then break out and head for the inside lane. At the next three changeovers the eight receivers jostle for the best position in the pack. The final (anchor) leg is usually reserved for the team's fastest 400m runner.

▲ Great Britain's Mark Hylton exchanges the baton with Du'aine Ladejo in a heat of the 4 x 400m at the 1996 Atlanta Games. Because relay teams make use of the squad system, with the entire squad either winning or losing, neither of these athletes was part of the quartet that won silver behind the U.S. in the final.

In the zone

Relay races, especially the 4 x 100m, are often won and lost in the changeover zone, where the baton is exchanged. This 66-ft. (20m)-long box is marked on the track, and the baton must be completely in the grip of the receiving athlete by the time his or her hand has left the zone. If not, the team is disqualified. The baton is swept either upward or downward into the receiver's hand, and runners must make sure that a large portion of the baton is presented to the receiver. A dropped baton does not lead to official disqualification but instead means that the team has no chance of winning because vital seconds have been lost.

◄ Gail Devers of the U.S. competes in the 100m hurdles at the Sydney Olympics. Devers overcame serious illness to become a three-time world champion in the 100m hurdles, as well as the winner of two Olympic golds in the 100m flat sprint. A pulled muscle in the hurdles semifinal forced her out of the Sydney Games, and she has yet to win an Olympic medal in her favored event.

▼ Athletes complete the water jump in heat three of the steeplechase at the 2000 Games. This heat produced the eventual gold medal winner, Reuben Kosgei of Kenya (right) and the bronze medalist, Morocco's Ali Ezzine (center).

Steeplechase

One of the few remaining track-and-field events for men only, the 3,000m steeplechase combines middle-distance speed and stamina with the task of clearing 28 hurdles and seven water jumps. These obstacles provide moments of high drama, with athletes stumbling and sometimes even falling. Steeplechasers use a 400m hurdling technique to clear the regular barriers, while many use the top of the water jump as a springboard to clear as much of the 12 ft. (3.66m) of water as possible. Kenya has dominated this event in recent years, winning gold in every Olympics since 1984.

LONG JUMP AND TRIPLE JUMP

Both the long jump and the triple jump begin with a fast, rhythmic sprint, followed by an explosive takeoff and one or a series of distance-covering moves before landing. Top Olympic long jumpers often double up successfully in the 100m sprint since the need for extreme acceleration and pace is similar. Triple jumpers have great speed too, but this must be balanced with a high level of control and a smooth rhythm in order to complete jumps that are long enough to earn an Olympic medal.

Runway, takeoff, landing

Olympic long jumpers take three qualifying jumps. The best eight athletes take a further three leaps in the final. Before a jump a competitor runs from a starting point at the far end of the 148-ft. (45-m)-long runway. From there, the jumper sprints forward, gradually moving into an upright position as he or she reaches top speed. Exploding off the take-off board, the jumper tries to cover as much distance through the air as possible before landing. Officials measure an attempt both electronically and by hand. The distance is calculated from the front edge of the take-off board to the closest mark made in the pit. For this reason jumpers try not to sit down when they land or to leave any mark in the sand behind where their feet have landed.

▲ Carl Lewis collects sand from the pit after winning the long jump in the 1996 Atlanta Games. Lewis narrowly made it into the American team and then only made it into the final on his last qualifying jump. But the reigning champion saved his best for the final, beating the world record holder, Mike Powell, in the process.

▲ Long jumpers sprint to the take-off board before pushing upward and forward from their take-off foot. The legs and arms are thrown forward, and upon landing the body is pulled through ahead of the feet and legs.

Increasing distances

As athletes have improved their training and abilities, the distances they have been able to long jump have increased. The 8m barrier—once believed to be impossible to achieve—is now regularly broken by male athletes. The top nine competitors in the men's long jump final in the Sydney Games, for example, all cleared more than 8m. Mike Powell of the U.S. holds the world record with a leap of 8.95m, recorded in 1991. The women's world record has stood for even longer, having been set in 1988 when Soviet athlete Galina Chistyakova jumped 7.52m. German athlete Heike Drechsler became the oldest female Olympic long jump champion in 2000 at the age of 35. Carl Lewis was the same age when he won his fourth consecutive long jump gold at the 1996 Games with a leap of 8.5m.

► Nigerian long jumper Chioma Ajunwa stands on top of the podium at the 1996 Olympics. Having had only three warm-up competitions before the Games, Ajunwa was a surprise winner. Her leap of 7.12m was 10cm ahead of Italy's Fiona May.

Take-off board

Modeling clay strip

▲ Both long and triple jumps are measured from the front of the take-off board. To maximize their chances of a winning jump athletes aim to plant their leading foot as close to the front of the board as possible.

▲ If the jumper's foot extends past the take-off line, it leaves an impression in the strip of soft modeling clay in front of the board. Officials will rule the attempt as a "no jump," and the athlete's distance is not recorded.

▶ British triple jumper Jonathan Edwards competes at the Sydney Olympics. Having set the world record of 18.29m in 1995, Edwards finally won an Olympic gold in 2000 at the age of 34. His jump of 17.71m was 24cm ahead of the silver medalist, Cuba's Yoel Garcia.

Triple jump

Although the women's triple jump only made its Olympic debut in 2000, the men's competition has been a feature of every modern Games. It was actually the first event of the 1896 Olympics, making the winner, James Connolly, the first gold medalist of the modern era. Traditionally known as a hop, step (or skip), and a jump, the event demands the highest level of technical discipline. Athletes must harness as much of their runway speed as possible into a series of distinct movements that are performed in a continuous flowing action. Connolly won the 1896 Games with a leap of 13.71m. Today male triple jumpers regularly surpass 17m, while the women's world record stands at 15.5m, set by Ukrainian athlete Inessa Kravets.

Anatomy of a triple jump

A triple jumper must build plenty of speed on the runway before taking off into the first stage of the jump, the hop. The knee of the take-off leg is driven upward and mostly forward, with the other leg swung back. As the hop phase ends the jumper stretches out his or her front leg to land on a flat foot. The step phase begins with the athlete swinging his or her trailing leg forward and driving off from the foot on the ground to take as long a stride as possible. The leading leg is kept bent at the knee so that the thigh is parallel to the ground. As the leading foot hits the ground the jump phase begins. The athlete drives off from the take-off leg, swings both arms forward, and brings the feet up and ahead of the body before landing in a similar way to a long jumper.

HIGH JUMP AND POLE VAULT

Two of the most spectacular events in track and field, the high jump and the pole vault have long been a feature of Olympic competitions for men, while the women's high jump first appeared in the Games in 1928, and the women's pole vault debuted in 2000. To succeed in either discipline requires great strength, speed, agility, and coordination. Athletes must time their run-up perfectly and then concentrate all of their energy and technique into a gravity-defying leap and then clearance of the bar.

▲ Russian high jumper Yelena Yelesina clears the bar during the 2000 Olympics in Sydney. The veteran athlete, who was the European high jump champion in 1989, cleared 2.01m to take the gold medal at the age of 30.

High jump

The high jump arena consists of a large area called the high jump runway and a bar resting on two supports attached to upright poles that stand approximately 13 ft. (4m) apart (see diagram). As the competition progresses, the height of the bar is raised, first by 2 in. (5cm) at a time and then by smaller increments. At every height jumpers have 90 seconds to complete each of their three attempts to clear the bar. Competitors are allowed to touch the bar and make it wobble, but it must not fall off the supports. Athletes who fail to clear the bar on three successive occasions must exit the competition. The winner is either the athlete who has completed a jump at a greater height than the other competitors or, if two or more jumpers have achieved the same height, the jumper who has had the fewest failures overall.

2

▲ The jumper's body turns as she travels headfirst over the bar. The jumper arches her back, aiming to clear the middle of the bar, which is its lowest point.

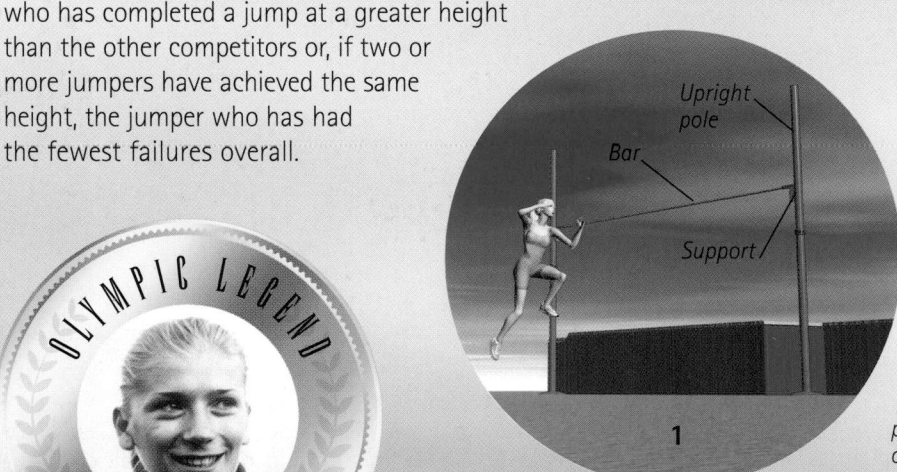

Upright pole

Bar

Support

1

◀ After a smooth, curved approach run the jumper plants her take-off foot firmly on the ground. The knee of the leading leg and the arms are driven upward as the athlete makes a powerful, explosive jump.

OLYMPIC LEGEND

Iolanda Balas (born 1936)

Nationality: *Romanian*
Games: *Melbourne 1956, Rome 1960, Tokyo 1964*
Event: *high jump*
Medals: *two gold*

High jump champions

The high jump has produced many famous Olympic champions among both its male and female competitors. One of the best was the double Olympic gold medalist Iolanda Balas, who broke the women's world record 14 times and was unbeaten during an astonishing 140 consecutive competitions between 1957 and 1967. West German jumper Ulrike Meyfarth—the winner of two Olympic high jump competitions 12 years apart (1972 and 1984)—was the first female jumper to clear 2m in Olympic competition. At the 1968 Games in Mexico City the U.S.'s Dick Fosbury revolutionized high jumping with a new technique that became known as the Fosbury flop (see p. 40). All of today's top high jumpers use this method to clear the bar.

▼ The jumper's hips rise as a result of the momentum created by the jump. The athlete looks over her shoulder to the far corner of the crash mat and tries to stay relaxed.

4

Crash mat

3

▲ As the jumper's hips pass over the bar, her legs are lifted to take them over as well. A good jump will see the jumper land on the crash mat on her back and shoulders.

▼ South African athlete Okkert Brits demonstrates just how much bending occurs in the pole during the take-off stage of the pole vault. Gripping the pole at its end, Brits is in the process of thrusting himself upward into an upside-down, vertical position.

Pole vault

Pole-vaulting is a breathtaking field event in which competitors use a strong, very flexible pole to leap heights of more than 5.5m (men) and 4.5m (women). A champion pole-vaulter needs to have the skills of a sprinter, a gymnast, and an acrobat. An attempt starts with the vaulter sprinting along a runway, building up great speed as he or she carries the pole in front, parallel to the ground. Expert timing is required to plant the pole, usually around 16 ft. (5m) in length, into the 8-in. (20-cm)-deep hole right in front of the vaulting uprights. The pole bends under the athlete's weight upon takeoff, and a good body position is required to allow the pole to straighten and carry the vaulter up toward the bar, which must be cleared without being knocked off. Ukrainian Sergei Bubka is considered the finest male vaulter of the modern era—in 1985 he became the first man to clear 6m in a competition.

◄ Danish pole-vaulter Marie Bagger competes in the women's final at the Sydney Games. As the pole unbends, Bagger is upside-down and vertical with her legs extended. Then, pivoting so that she is facing the bar, Bagger pushes off from the pole and brings her arms over to clear the bar.

1988 Sergei Bubka 5.9m

1968 Bob Seagren 5.4m

1956 Bob Richards 4.56m

1908 Edward Cooke and Albert Gilbert (tie) 3.71m

1896 William Hoyt 3.3m

▲ The men's Olympic pole vault record has risen dramatically over the years. It is currently held by Jean Galfione of France. The world record stands at an astonishing 6.14m, set in 1994 by the great Sergei Bubka.

33

HAMMER AND SHOT PUT

Two of the most extreme power events in track and field, the hammer throw and the shot put both call for explosive strength. Shot-putters and hammer throwers spend long sessions in the gym to develop the right muscles and physique. Yet both events require technical discipline and deep concentration in order to perfect the exact body movements and rhythm needed to throw medal-winning distances.

◀ Finnish hammer thrower Olli-Pekka Karjalainen maintains his rhythm as he spins in the circle and winds up to complete his throw.

The hammer throw
The men's hammer throw first appeared in the Olympics in 1900, although it took another 100 years before the women's event made its Olympic debut in Sydney. The hammer itself is a metal ball attached to a handle by a chain that measures around 4 ft. (1.2m) in length. The men's hammer weighs 16 lbs. (7.26kg), and the women's weighs 8.8 lbs (4kg). It is thrown from a 6.8-ft. (2.1m)-wide circle that is surrounded at the back and sides by a large safety cage.

1

2

3

◀ Poland scored a men's and women's double win in the hammer at the Sydney Games, with Kamila Skolimowska (left) and Szymon Ziolkowski winning gold. Skolimowska's throw of 71.16m set a new Olympic record.

◀ Gripping the handle with both hands, a thrower starts at the back of the circle, spinning the hammer around his or her head (1). To build momentum the thrower launches into three or four powerful turns across the circle, whirling the hammer around in a circular motion (2). The hammer is released so that it flies forward and upward at an ideal angle of around 45°, reaching a speed of up to 68 mph (110km/h) (3).

Equal weights, different distances

In both the shot put and the hammer throw athletes take three preliminary throws, with the best eight throwers and putters granted an additional three attempts. The hammer is the same weight as the shot, yet the fact that it is on a chain allows athletes to propel it much farther. The men's shot put world record is 23.12m, recorded by American Randy Barnes in 1990. The world record for the men's hammer is 86.74m. It was set in 1986 by the Soviet athlete Yuriy Sedykh and is one of the longest-standing track-and-field records. Releasing the hammer at exactly the right point is key to success. Until 1958 the fan-shaped landing area was at an angle of 90°. The reduction of the angle to 40° in 1970 forced throwers to increase their accuracy.

▶ *Arsi Harju of Finland roars in triumph after releasing his gold-medal-winning put of 21.29m in the second round of the men's competition at the Sydney Olympics. Harju's gold was Finland's first medal of the 2000 Games.*

▶ *Connie Price-Smith of the U.S. takes time to cradle the shot and perfect her starting position before powering across the circle to complete a put. Price-Smith competed in four consecutive Olympics between 1988 and 2000.*

The shot put

From a 6.8-ft. (2.1m)-diameter circle equipped with a 4-in. (10cm)-high stopboard at the front, a shot-putter must propel the shot with one arm so that it falls in the 40°, fan-shaped landing area. The shot is usually a solid metal ball made of copper or bronze, weighing 16 lbs. (7.26kg) in the men's competition and 8.8 lbs (4kg) in the women's. The shot is cradled in the neck using the fingers and then released with a powerful extension of the arm.

Generating speed and power

Shot-putters use one of two methods to generate speed and power across the circle. The rotational method sees a shot-putter spinning around, almost like a discus thrower (see pp. 36–37), using the foot on his or her non-throwing side as a pivot. The linear throw is often known as the O'Brien technique, after the American double-Olympic gold medalist Parry O'Brien. Using this method in the 1950s, he became the first man to throw more than 18m and, later, the first to exceed 19m. By starting a throw facing the back of the circle and then using a 180° turn to shift his weight to the front of the circle, he improved the world record 16 times.

▲ *A stunning women's shot put contest at the Sydney Olympics saw Belarussian Yanina Karolchik save the best throw of her life for the last round. Karolchik threw 20.56m to win gold ahead of Larisa Peleshenko and Astrid Kumbernuss.*

DISCUS AND JAVELIN

The discus and javelin were events found in the ancient Olympics—the discus has appeared in every modern Olympics and the javelin in each one since 1908. Both events require power, speed, coordination, and technical precision. The angle at which the discus or javelin is released is key to success. Competitors in both events take three throws when qualifying, with the eight who throw farthest given an additional three attempts in the final.

▲ *American Al Oerter won four consecutive Olympic gold medals in the discus. His last victory, shown here, was at the 1968 Mexico City Games.*

Moving in circles

The discus competition takes place in an 8.2-ft.-wide throwing circle surrounded by a protective cage. Throwers must enter and leave the circle from the back, and the discus must first hit the ground and be completely inside the 40° landing area for the throw to be considered legal. Discus throwers build rhythm with a number of preliminary swings before traveling across the circle, usually completing one-and-a-half body turns. With each turn the discus builds up more speed—the greater the speed upon release, the farther the discus will tend to fly.

▶ *The athlete braces the non-throwing side of their body to provide a solid platform for the rest of the body to move against. The throwing arm then starts to whip around.*

◀ *German athlete Ilke Wyludda won the 1996 Olympics women's discus event with a throw of 69.66m. She was joined on the podium by the silver-winning Russian Natalya Sadova and the Belarussian Ellina Zvereva, who went on to win gold in 2000.*

◀ *The discus thrower turns, moving across the circle with legs bent and the upper body and head upright. A right-handed thrower pivots around his or her right foot so that the left foot lands close to the front of the circle.*

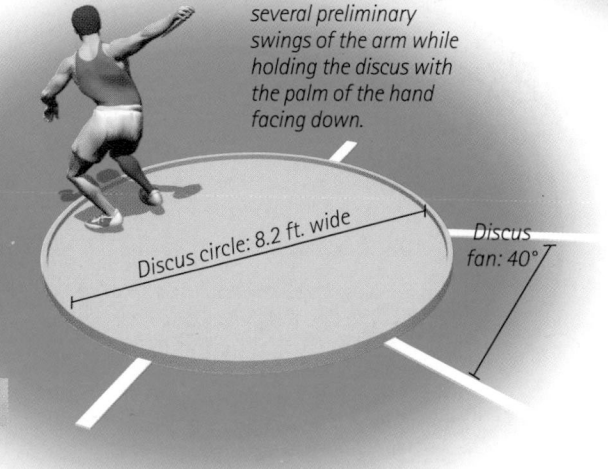

◀ *At the start of a discus throw the athlete builds up momentum by making several preliminary swings of the arm while holding the discus with the palm of the hand facing down.*

Discus circle: 8.2 ft. wide

Discus fan: 40°

Angle of attack

The discus weighs 4.4 lbs. (2kg) in the men's competition and 2.2 lbs. (1kg) in the women's. The discus is shaped to generate lift as it flies through the air, provided it is released at the correct angle—between 34°–37°. Coordinating the precise body, arm, and hand positions to achieve this angle while generating explosive power is extremely difficult and depends on an athlete perfecting the technique through hundreds of training throws. The qualifying standards for the 2004 Olympics are set at 64.6m for men and 63.4m for women.

▶ With shoulders facing the front, the thrower releases the discus from the front of his or her hand, pressing down on its leading edge with the fingers to make sure that it spins away at the correct angle.

From runway to takeoff

Javelin throwers begin a throw at the end of a runway that is at least 98 ft. (30m) long. Over 10–12 strides they build up speed, making sure that the javelin is level and just above shoulder height. The next step is to transfer as much of this speed as possible to the javelin—by drawing the throwing arm back, planting both feet on the ground, and suddenly stopping the run. The javelin is pulled through with a controlled but powerful whipping motion. Ideally released at an angle of around 40° upward, the javelin flies away at a speed of more than 62 mph (100km/h).

The javelin

Ancient Olympians used a looped leather strap to propel an olive branch javelin great distances. Modern throwers rely on speed, power, and perfect coordination in the most spectacular of the throwing events. The javelin must be thrown overhand, and officials mark the point where it first touches the ground. Although the javelin does not have to stick in the grass, its tip must land first in order for the throw to be legal. Javelin techniques improved throughout the 1900s to the point, in 1984, when East German athlete Uwe Hohn threw an astonishing 104.8m. In 1986, to decrease distances, the javelin's center of gravity and gripping point were changed. However, the top male throwers can exceed 85–90m if conditions are good. For example, Jan Zelezny won the 2000 Games with a throw of 90.17m.

◀ Czech athlete Jan Zelezny dominated Olympic javelin competitions during the 1990s. The son of javelin-throwing parents, Zelezny won Olympic silver in 1988 and three consecutive golds at the 1992, 1996, and 2000 games.

Javelin is between 8.5–8.9 ft. (2.6–2.7m) long and weighs 1.75 lbs. (800g)

▼ A javelin thrower builds up speed along the runway before planting both feet on the ground and using fast body and arm movements to pull the javelin past the body. After release the thrower's right leg comes forward, hits the ground, and acts like a brake to stop the athlete from traveling over the stopboard.

Stopboard

MULTI-SPORTS EVENTS

Four Summer Olympic track-and-field events demand excellence in more than one discipline. These multi-sports events are regarded by many competitors and spectators as the greatest challenges of the Games. Each multi-sports event requires athletes to master a range of contrasting techniques and calls on all of their fitness, stamina, and mental strength.

▲ *American decathlete Bob Mathias was unbeaten in all of the 11 decathlons he entered, including two Olympic competitions. In the 1952 Games he won by 912 points—the largest winning margin in Olympic decathlon history.*

Heptathlon

From 1964 to 1980 women competed in the Olympic pentathlon, which consisted of five events: the long jump, shot put, high jump, 80m hurdles, and 200m sprint. In 1984 this was replaced by the seven-event heptathlon, which is held over two consecutive days. An athlete's times in the track events and her best throw or jump in each field event are converted into points using a scoring table. The athlete with the most points wins. For many the heptathlon is considered to be the ultimate challenge in women's track and field and one that American legend Jackie Joyner-Kersee certainly rose to. A string of amazing performances during the 1980s and early 1990s culminated in two Olympic gold medals. Her score of 7,291 points at the 1988 Seoul Games remains a world and Olympic record.

◀ *British decathlete Daley Thompson became only the second Olympian to win successive decathlon golds, in Moscow in 1980 and Los Angeles in 1984.*

OLYMPIC LEGEND
Jackie Joyner-Kersee (born 1962)

Nationality: *American*
Games: *Los Angeles 1984, Seoul 1988, Barcelona 1992, Atlanta 1996*
Events: *heptathlon, long jump*
Medals: *three gold, one silver, two bronze*

Decathlon

The men's decathlon is one of the most popular events in the Olympic track-and-field program. As the competitors vie for the gold medal over two days and ten disciplines, the excitement mounts. Just like in the heptathlon, performances are converted into points. The athletes compete in five events per day, with the competition reaching its climax on the track with the final event, the 1,500m run. Both the decathlon and heptathlon place enormous strains on an athlete's mind and body. A typical day can last as long as ten hours, and competitors have to remain focused and ready to perform at all times. A small, persistent injury or a poor result in an earlier event must be put aside if they are to recover and win a medal.

▶ Swiss triathlete Brigitte McMahon competes in all three elements of the women's triathlon at the 2000 Games: swimming in Sydney harbor, followed by cycling and, finally, the road race around the streets of the city. In a thrilling finale McMahon broke away from local triathlete Michellie Jones in the last 100m to win gold in a time of two hours and 40 seconds.

▼ British heptathlete Denise Lewis clears the high jump bar during the Sydney Olympics heptathlon. Lewis managed to complete the two-day event despite having several injuries and triumphed to win gold ahead of Russia's Yelena Prokhorova.

Triathlon

The first major triathlon competition of any type took place in 1974. The event, one of the newest of all Olympic sports, made its Olympic debut in Sydney and is one of only a handful of sports in which male and female athletes compete at the same time. At the Olympic level the triathlon begins with the group start of a 1.5km swim, which is followed by a 40km cycle ride and then a grueling 10km run. The event is nonstop, and a quick and effective changeover between disciplines is essential to success. Competitors hone their swimming, cycling, and running styles carefully since any improvement in technique, multiplied by the large distances they must cover, can make a great difference to their final placement in this energy-sapping event.

◀ Stephanie Cook of Great Britain competes in the equestrian jumping discipline of the women's modern pentathlon, which made its Olympic debut in 2000. Cook went on to become the first gold medalist in the event.

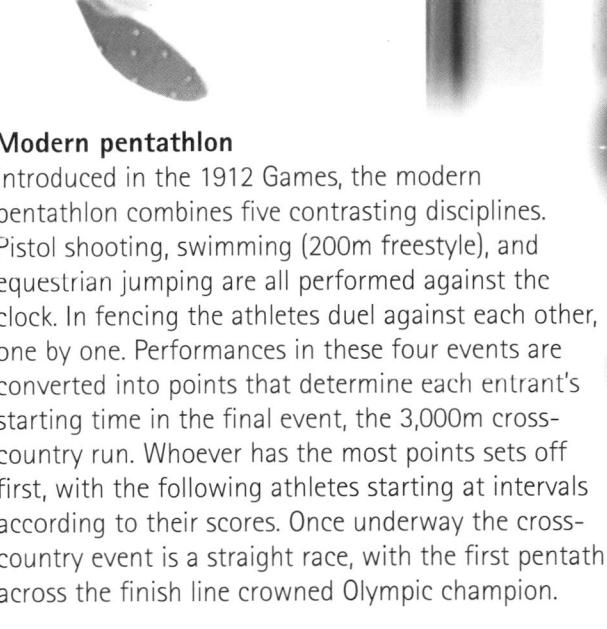

Modern pentathlon

Introduced in the 1912 Games, the modern pentathlon combines five contrasting disciplines. Pistol shooting, swimming (200m freestyle), and equestrian jumping are all performed against the clock. In fencing the athletes duel against each other, one by one. Performances in these four events are converted into points that determine each entrant's starting time in the final event, the 3,000m cross-country run. Whoever has the most points sets off first, with the following athletes starting at intervals according to their scores. Once underway the cross-country event is a straight race, with the first pentathlete across the finish line crowned Olympic champion.

Heptathlon: 100m hurdles, high jump, shot put, 200m, long jump, javelin, 800m

Decathlon: 100m, long jump, shot put, high jump, 400m, 110m hurdles, discus, pole vault, javelin, 1,500m

Triathlon: 1.5km swim, 40km cycle ride, 10km run

Modern pentathlon: Shooting, fencing, 200m swim, jumping, 3,000m run

MEXICO CITY 1968

When Mexico City was awarded the 1968 Summer Olympics, a major concern was its location. At an altitude of 7,200 ft. (2,200m), the air contains 30 percent less oxygen than at sea level. Competitors in endurance events suffered, and recorded times were slow. In contrast, shorter-distance events and explosive power disciplines, such as jumping and weight lifting, prospered, and a total of 34 world and 38 Olympic records were set.

▲ *One of the posters for the Games depicted a pattern inspired by the ancient Aztecs, rulers of a large empire in the region in the 1400s and 1500s.*

◄ *Mexican hurdler Enriqueta Basilio de Sotelo holds the Olympic torch at the opening ceremony of the 1968 Games. She was the first woman to light the Olympic flame.*

Troubled times

The Mexico City Olympics were staged during a time of great unrest in parts of the world. South Africa was barred from the games for its policy of apartheid, racial tensions were high in the U.S., and Soviet tanks had invaded Czechoslovakia two months before the opening ceremony. Czech gymnast Vera Caslavska, a critic of the Soviet invasion, had gone into hiding for a period before the Games but emerged triumphant to dominate the women's gymnastics events, winning four gold medals and two silvers.

▶ *American athlete Dick Fosbury delighted the crowd in Mexico City by unveiling an innovative style of high jumping. The Fosbury flop, as it became known, won him the Olympic gold medal.*

▶ *American sprinters Tommie Smith and John Carlos won gold and bronze in the 200m. On the podium they raised their black-gloved fists as a protest against racism in the U.S. Both men were expelled from the Olympic Village. Australian silver medalist, Peter Norman, wore a badge in support.*

Talking points

American athletes provided many of the Mexico City Games' major talking points. Dick Fosbury won the high jump with a radical new technique, and Wyomia Tyus became the first woman to win consecutive Olympic golds in the 100m. The men's field event program was dominated by athletes from Eastern Europe and the Soviet Union, but Al Oerter of the U.S. grabbed the headlines with a record fourth gold medal in the discus (see p. 36). Tommie Smith broke the world record in the 200m, yet he is remembered more for the "black power" salute he made alongside his teammate, John Carlos.

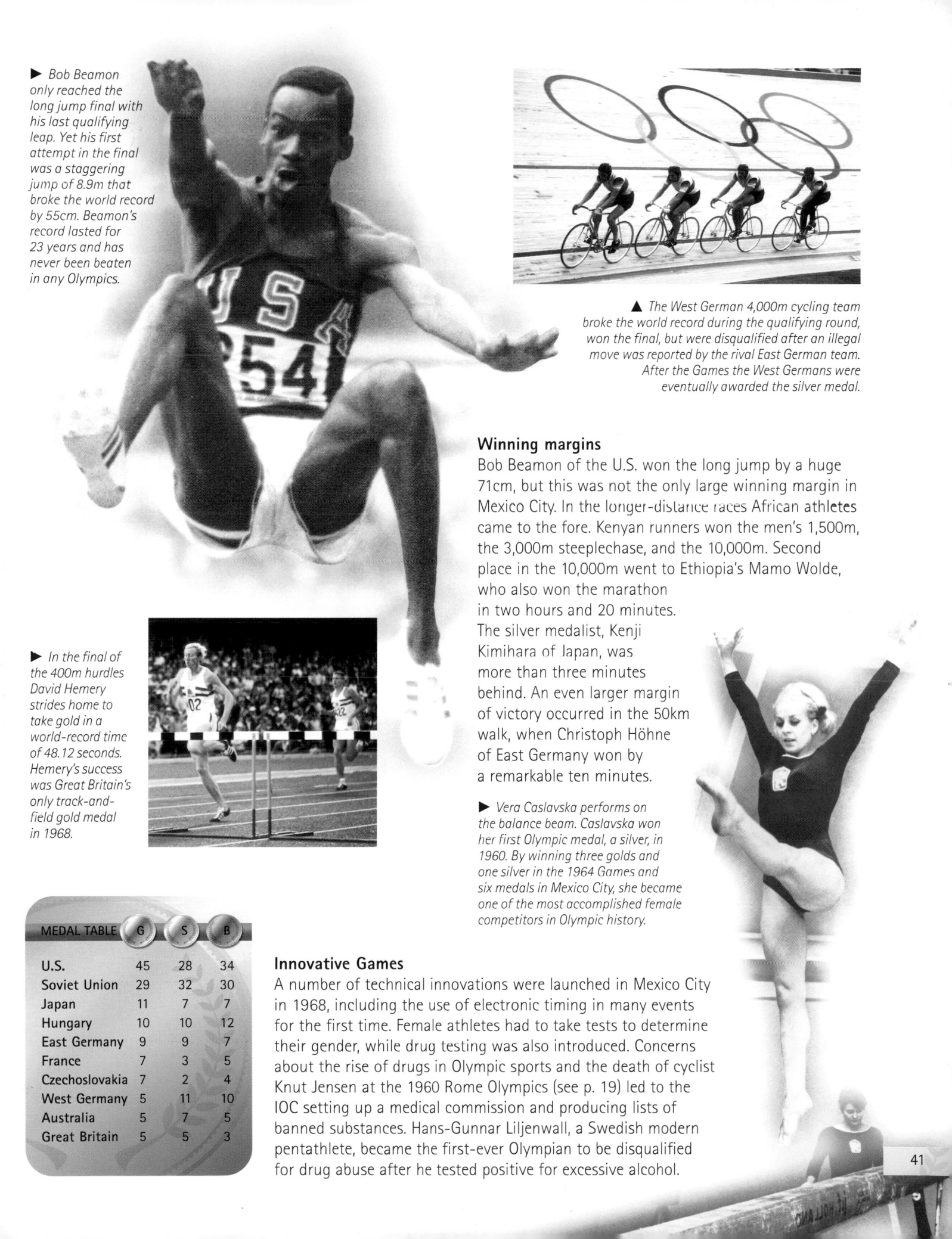

► Bob Beamon only reached the long jump final with his last qualifying leap. Yet his first attempt in the final was a staggering jump of 8.9m that broke the world record by 55cm. Beamon's record lasted for 23 years and has never been beaten in any Olympics.

▲ The West German 4,000m cycling team broke the world record during the qualifying round, won the final, but were disqualified after an illegal move was reported by the rival East German team. After the Games the West Germans were eventually awarded the silver medal.

► In the final of the 400m hurdles David Hemery strides home to take gold in a world-record time of 48.12 seconds. Hemery's success was Great Britain's only track-and-field gold medal in 1968.

Winning margins

Bob Beamon of the U.S. won the long jump by a huge 71cm, but this was not the only large winning margin in Mexico City. In the longer-distance races African athletes came to the fore. Kenyan runners won the men's 1,500m, the 3,000m steeplechase, and the 10,000m. Second place in the 10,000m went to Ethiopia's Mamo Wolde, who also won the marathon in two hours and 20 minutes. The silver medalist, Kenji Kimihara of Japan, was more than three minutes behind. An even larger margin of victory occurred in the 50km walk, when Christoph Höhne of East Germany won by a remarkable ten minutes.

► Vera Caslavska performs on the balance beam. Caslavska won her first Olympic medal, a silver, in 1960. By winning three golds and one silver in the 1964 Games and six medals in Mexico City, she became one of the most accomplished female competitors in Olympic history.

MEDAL TABLE	G	S	B
U.S.	45	28	34
Soviet Union	29	32	30
Japan	11	7	7
Hungary	10	10	12
East Germany	9	9	7
France	7	3	5
Czechoslovakia	7	2	4
West Germany	5	11	10
Australia	5	7	5
Great Britain	5	5	3

Innovative Games

A number of technical innovations were launched in Mexico City in 1968, including the use of electronic timing in many events for the first time. Female athletes had to take tests to determine their gender, while drug testing was also introduced. Concerns about the rise of drugs in Olympic sports and the death of cyclist Knut Jensen at the 1960 Rome Olympics (see p. 19) led to the IOC setting up a medical commission and producing lists of banned substances. Hans-Gunnar Liljenwall, a Swedish modern pentathlete, became the first-ever Olympian to be disqualified for drug abuse after he tested positive for excessive alcohol.

SWIMMING

In 1896 three sailors dived into the chilly waters of the Bay of Zea, off the coast of Greece, to complete a swim of approximately 328 ft. (100m) back to shore. From this humble start Olympic swimming has blossomed to become one of the most popular attractions of the entire Games. Events at the aquatic center are always a sellout because spectators savor the glamour, drama, and excitement that Olympic swimming generates.

▲ Aleksandr Popov is Russia's most successful swimmer. He dominated the freestyle sprint events during the 1990s, winning four Olympic gold medals and five silvers.

Into the pool

Early Olympic swimming events took place in rivers and lakes, as well as in the sea. The 1908 Games featured a giant 328-ft. (100-m)-long pool, but modern Olympic pools have a standard length of 164 ft. (50m) and a width great enough for eight swimming lanes separated by lane ropes. Races are held over a wide range of distances, from the dynamic 50m sprint to the lung-busting 800m for women and 1,500m for men. The sprints at 50m and 100m are speed events, requiring a swimmer's maximum pace from start to finish. The longer-distance races require the swimmer to decide on a strategy—either to swim the entire race evenly or to hold some energy in reserve in order to swim a faster second half.

▶ Dutch swimmer Inge de Bruijn waves to the crowd after cruising through her heat of the women's 100m butterfly in Sydney, one of three events that she won there.

▲ Australia's Scott Miller shows an excellent starting technique as he dives off his starting block during a heat of the 200m butterfly at the 1996 Games.

Different strokes

Four different swimming strokes are featured in the Olympic competition: breaststroke, backstroke, butterfly, and freestyle. Technically, freestyle means any stroke that the swimmer chooses, but in practice it means the front crawl—the fastest of the strokes. The crawl, butterfly, and breaststroke all start with a forward dive from the starting blocks, after which competitors can swim up to 49 ft. (15m) underwater before coming to the surface. A false start in any swimming event results in disqualification. In the breaststroke the swimmer's head must surface during every stroke. At the end of one length of the pool freestyle and backstroke swimmers may touch the wall with any part of their bodies, and so most execute a tumble turn, performing a somersault in the water and pushing off of the wall with their feet. Breaststroke and butterfly swimmers must touch the end of the pool with both hands before turning for the next length.

Relays and medleys

Relays involve teams of four swimmers, each of whom uses the freestyle crawl stroke to swim 100m in the 400m relay or 200m in the 800m relay. Swimmers must not leave their blocks more than 0.03 seconds before their teammate has touched the wall, or they are disqualified. Medley events feature all four strokes. In the 200m individual medley competitors swim 50m of the butterfly followed by the same distance of the backstroke, breaststroke, and, finally, freestyle. The order is the same for the 400m individual medley, with competitors swimming 100m of each stroke. The medley relay features all four strokes, but each is swum by a different swimmer—starting with the backstroke and then the breaststroke, butterfly, and freestyle.

▲ Swimming legend Mark Spitz launches himself forward out of the water on his way to winning the men's 200m butterfly at the 1972 Olympics. This victory was only one of seven for the American at the Games—the largest-ever individual gold medal haul at a single Olympics in any sport.

Great champions

Swimming offers a wide range of events, and champion swimmers frequently come away from an Olympics with more than one medal. Although each stroke requires a dramatically different technique, many great swimmers have mastered several—often the butterfly and freestyle—to win Olympic gold in different stroke events. Australia's Ian Thorpe and the Netherlands' Inge de Bruijn managed this feat at the Sydney Games. Other great champions have shown surprising longevity to win medals at three or more Olympics. Australia's Dawn Fraser became the first woman to defend an Olympic swimming title when she won the 100m freestyle at the 1960 Rome Games. She went on to win the event for a third time in 1964, a first for a swimmer of either sex.

▲ Australia's Ian Thorpe pushes off of the pool wall at the start of a 100m backstroke race.

▼ Kieren Perkins of Australia breathes to the side while powering his way through the 1,500m freestyle at the Atlanta Games. Perkins was a master at this event, winning gold in 1992 and 1996 and silver in 2000.

OLYMPIC LEGEND

Dawn Fraser (born 1937)

Nationality: Australian
Games: Melbourne 1956, Rome 1960, Tokyo 1964
Events: 100m and 400m freestyle, 4 x 100m freestyle relay, 4 x 100m medley relay
Medals: four gold, four silver

▼ *A diver soars into the air during practice for the women's 10m platform competition at the 1996 Atlanta Olympics.*

DIVING, WATER POLO, AND SYNCHRONIZED SWIMMING

Swimming is not the only sport to entertain spectators at an Olympic aquatic center. Diving requires athleticism and split-second timing, as does synchronized swimming. In both events judges mark the technical and artistic prowess of competitors. In contrast, water polo is an all-action team sport played in the pool.

Diving—springboard and platform

Diving was one of the first Olympic sports to feature events for both men and women. Men's diving debuted in 1904, while diving for women was introduced eight years later. Today Olympic diving competitions are held at two heights: the springboard dive is set at 10 ft. (3m) above the pool's surface and the platform dive at 33 ft. (10m) above the water. Divers compete in a preliminary round, with the top 18 progressing to the semifinal. The 12 best then compete in the final. In each round competitors perform a number of dives, which they must select from the dozens of different dives possible. Synchronized events—where two teammates perform the same dive at the same time—made their first Olympic appearance in Sydney in 2000.

▶ *This is an inward one-and-a-half somersault dive, with the diver performing the somersault in a tuck position with her knees brought up to her chest. It has a degree of difficulty of 1.9, making it a middle-ranking dive in the 3m springboard event.*

◀ *Na Li and Xue Sang of China hold their bodies in almost perfect symmetry during a synchronized dive at the Sydney Games. The pair won the 10m platform event by a huge margin of more than 30 points and also won gold in the 3m springboard competition.*

Judging and marking

Dives are judged on many elements, including the quality of execution of the moves in the air and the cleanness of entry into the water. In individual events divers are marked by seven judges. The highest and lowest scores are removed, leaving five that are added together. Each dive has a degree of difficulty that is expressed as a number—the more complex the dive, the higher the number. A diver's score is multiplied by the degree of difficulty and then multiplied by 0.6 to give the final score. This formula rewards divers who gamble on a more challenging dive but also gives the chance of a competitive score to those who perform simpler dives almost perfectly.

Water polo

Part of the Olympics since 1900, water polo is the longest-running team sport of the modern era, but only in 2000 was a women's competition introduced. It is a seven-on-seven game in which players try to propel a floating ball into their opponents' 10-ft. (3-m)-wide and 3-ft. (90-cm)-high goal. Players can use any part of their bodies to nudge the ball along the surface of the water or to pass it to teammates, but they must not punch the ball or drag it below the surface. Only the goalkeeper is allowed to place both hands on the ball at the same time. Once a team takes possession of the ball, it has 35 seconds to score a goal—otherwise the ball passes to the opposing team. Fouls are divided into two classes, ordinary and major. Committing three major fouls sees a player excluded from the game. Throughout a game players are constantly in motion, either swimming to get into an attacking position or to defend or treading water to stay afloat. To shoot, players propel themselves upward to get as much of their bodies out of the water as possible. This helps generate a powerful throw.

▲ Hungary's Tamas Marcz overtakes Alexander Erychov of Russia during the men's water polo final in 2000. Hungary won 13–6 to claim their seventh Olympic gold medal in the event.

▶ Italian goalkeeper Francesco Attolico makes a save in Sydney. Goalkeepers are the only players who are allowed to touch the bottom of the pool in water polo.

Synchronized swimming

Originating in Canada and the U.S., synchronized swimming made its Olympic debut in Los Angeles in 1984. Today the sport involves pairs or teams of eight swimmers performing routines made up of many different moves, all set to music that is played both above and under the water. Competitors must execute a technical routine and a freestyle routine—both within a time limit. In the technical section swimmers perform a series of specific moves in a set order, while the freestyle section allows them to produce their own choreographed routines, often featuring spectacular and graceful figures and moves. Swimmers can stay underwater for as long as 60 seconds per sequence and must coordinate their actions perfectly with their teammates. Performances are marked by ten judges, who are divided into two panels. One panel focuses on technical merit, the other on artistic merit. Synchronized swimmers make their routines appear effortless and flowing, but in reality, a lot of hard work, strength, and stamina are required.

▲ The French synchronized swimming team in action during its freestyle routine at the Sydney Olympics. Despite scoring well, the French were beaten to the bronze medal by Canada.

▶ Here the French team performs a graceful freestyle move during a practice session in Sydney.

45

ROWING, SAILING, AND CANOE/KAYAK

Outside on the water three distinct sets of events attract large Olympic crowds who watch in awe at the extremely high levels of endurance, strength, and technical skill on display. Rowing and sailing made their debuts at the Paris Games of 1900, while canoe/kayak first appeared as a demonstration sport at the 1920 Antwerp Olympics before being given full-medal status in Berlin in 1936.

▲ The women's K-4 500m kayak competition gets underway at the Sydney Games. K-4 refers to the number of paddlers in each boat. There are also K-1 and K-2 competitions at the Olympics, for single paddlers and pairs.

▲ The men's coxless four crew from Great Britain power through a heat at the 2000 Games on their way to an historic fifth Olympic gold medal for Steve Redgrave (third from the front) and a third gold for Matthew Pinsent (front).

Rowing
One of the toughest of all endurance sports, rowing at the Olympics is held over a 2,000m-long course. Rowers push their bodies to the ultimate limit, and in the final stages of a race—despite being close to exhaustion—they reach astonishing speeds of up to 33 ft. (10m) per second (22 mph/36km/h). In crew events for two, four, or eight people rowers must synchronize their timing and match the power of the rest of the crew to ensure a smooth and fast row.

▼ The all-powerful women's coxed eight from Romania on their way to gold in Sydney, repeating their feat of 1996.

Sculling and sweeping
Rowing is one of the larger sports featured in the Olympics. In Athens in 2004 more than 500 rowers will compete in one dozen different events. There are two broad categories: sculling events, where competitors use two oars each, and sweeping-oar events, where they grip a single oar with both hands. Some events are coxed. This means that an additional person, called the coxswain, sits at the stern (back) of the boat, controlling the pace of the crew and steering. The largest boats hold nine people in the coxed eights, which is usually considered the blue ribbon rowing event. In all the events a series of qualifying heats is held to determine the lineup of the six-boat final.

Canoe/kayak

Canoes and kayaks are similar craft, but they are raced using different paddling techniques. Canoeists race in a kneeling position and use a single-bladed paddle, while kayakers race in a sitting position, using a paddle with a blade at both ends. Sprint events are held for both canoes and kayaks on flat water (still water) courses of different distances. Women race over 500m in the sprints, while men compete over 500m and 1,000m. Canoes and kayaks are also used in white-water slalom events. In these events competitors power their way through turbulent, rapidly flowing water. Their goal is to pass through a series of between 20 and 25 gates, which are set out over a specially designed course, in the shortest possible time.

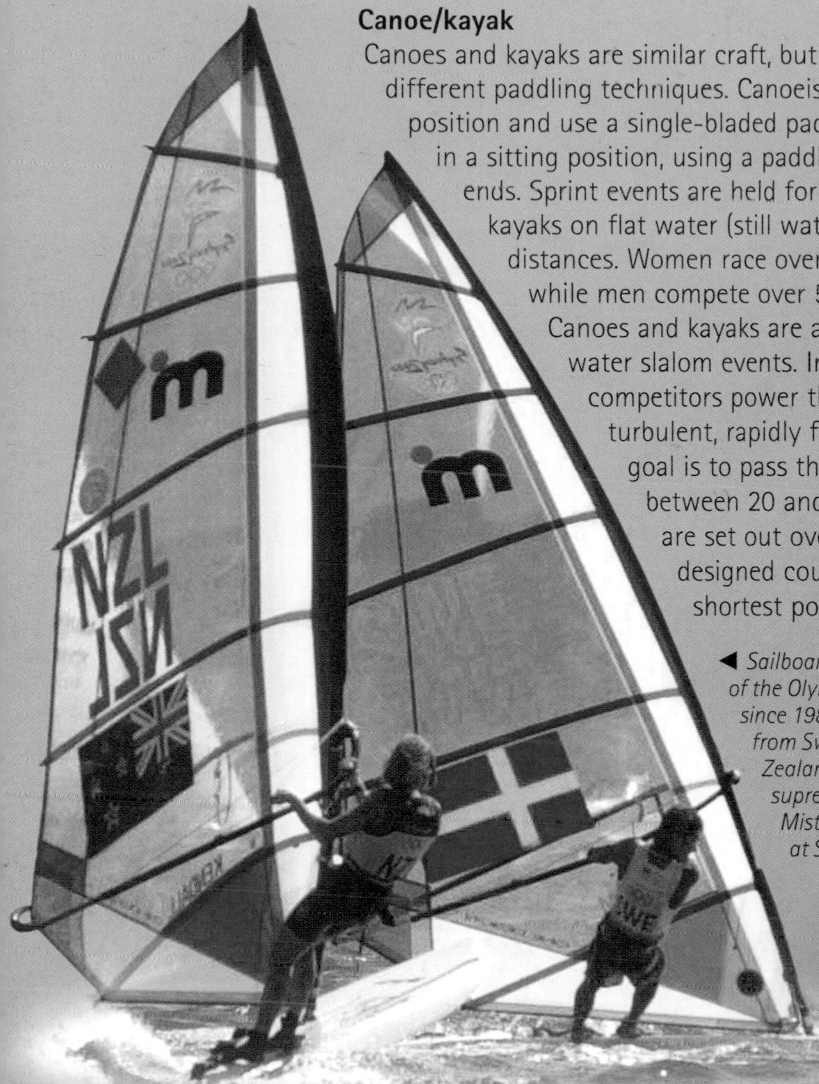

◄ *Sailboarding has been part of the Olympic sailing program since 1984. Here sailboarders from Sweden and New Zealand battle for supremacy in the Mistral class event at Sydney 2000.*

▲ *Steering hard, Italian kayaker Pierpaolo Ferrazzi thrusts his paddle into the fast-flowing water of the white-water kayak course in Sydney. Ferrazzi, who won gold in this event's Olympic debut in 1992, won a bronze in 2000 behind Germany's Thomas Schmidt and Paul Ratcliffe of Great Britain.*

Sailing

A range of sailing events is found at the Olympics, each for a different class of boat. There were nine types of craft at the Sydney Games, including single-sailor boats, such as the Finn and the Europe, as well as two-person 49ers and three-person Ynglings. Some events are restricted to either men or women, while others, such as the Tornado class, are open to both sexes. In almost all events competitors take part in a series of races (11 in most classes, 16 in the 49er event) in which all the competing craft race together. Points are awarded according to finishing positions, with one point for first place, two for second place, and so on. The boat with the lowest-point score over the series of races is the winner.

OLYMPIC LEGEND

Vyacheslav Ivanov (born 1938)

Nationality: *Russian*
Games: *Melbourne 1956, Rome 1960, Tokyo 1964*
Events: *single sculls rowing*
Medals: *three gold*

◄ *Great Britain's Ben Ainslie competes in the one-person Laser class at the 2000 Olympics. Ainslie won the competition, held in Sydney harbor, achieving even better than his silver medal in Atlanta in 1996.*

 # SEOUL 1988

The second Summer Games to be held in Asia, the Seoul Olympics were marked by the return of many nations that had boycotted the Games of 1980 or 1984. Only North Korea, Nicaragua, Cuba, and Ethiopia stayed away. The Games are remembered for their unprecedented levels of security and for the highest-profile drugs disqualification of the modern era. However, the Seoul Olympics were also a well-run showcase for South Korean culture, and they were marked by some outstanding performances.

▲ The official poster of the 1988 Games portrayed a runner holding the Olympic torch, symbolizing the Olympic ideals of harmony and progress.

◀ Ben Johnson salutes the crowd after winning the 100m sprint and breaking the world record with a time of 9.79 seconds. Within days he would be disgraced and stripped of his medal.

◀▲ In 1936 Korean athlete Sohn Kee-chung had been forced to enter the Olympic marathon using a Japanese name because his home country was occupied by Japan. He won the gold medal. More than 50 years later, at the age of 76, Sohn was chosen to carry the Olympic torch into the stadium to open the Seoul Games, a dramatic and emotional moment.

The Ben Johnson scandal

When the world's top sprinters lined up for the 100m final in excellent condition, something special was expected. What happened came as a shock to the worldwide audience. Canadian sprinter Ben Johnson demolished his top-class opponents, including Carl Lewis and Linford Christie, clocking a sensational world-record time to win gold easily. Johnson's glory, however, was short-lived. He returned a positive drugs test for a banned steroid, stanozolol. Despite protests, Johnson was stripped of both his gold medal and the world record, and he received a two-year ban from the International Association of Athletics Federations (IAAF). This became a life ban when he tested positive again in 1993. Johnson's disqualification was the highest-profile drugs case of the ten made at the Seoul Olympics.

New arrivals

In Seoul tennis made its first appearance at the Olympics since 1924. The surprise winner of the men's tournament was Czechoslovakia's Milosav Mecir, who beat Tim Mayotte and the favorite Stefan Edberg on his way to the gold medal. Table tennis (Ping-Pong™) was a new sport at the Games and proved to be very popular. South Korea won the women's doubles and claimed gold and silver in the men's singles, while China won the women's singles and the men's doubles. Women's sprint cycling and team archery also debuted, while tae kwon do appeared as a demonstration sport.

▼ American diver Greg Louganis hits his head on the board during the 3m springboard competition. Despite being shaken, Louganis went on to win the event, along with the 10m platform dive, a double he had also achieved in the 1984 Games.

◀ In the women's final of the first Olympic tennis competition for 64 years West German star Steffi Graf won gold by beating Gabriela Sabatini of Argentina 6-3, 6-3.

▼ Jackie Joyner-Kersee of the U.S. on her way to winning the long jump gold medal. Joyner-Kersee also won the heptathlon, while her sister-in-law, Florence Griffith-Joyner, won three golds and one silver on the track.

Record-breaking women

There were many outstanding and record-breaking female performances in the Seoul Olympics. Swedish fencer Kerstin Palm became the first woman to compete in seven Olympics, while East Germany's Christa Luding-Rothenburger's silver in cycling made her the only athlete ever to win Winter and Summer Olympic medals in the same year—in the Calgary Winter Games seven months earlier she had claimed gold and silver in speed skating. In track and field the most dominant performance came from Soviet shot-putter Natalya Lisovskaya. All six of her throws were better than any other competitor's.

In the pool

In 1984 American swimmer Matt Biondi had won an Olympic gold medal as part of the men's 4 x 100m freestyle relay team. Four years later Biondi returned to the Olympic competition in astonishing form, winning five gold medals, a silver, and a bronze. His defeat in the 200m freestyle final came as a shock. Australian surfer and swimmer Duncan Armstrong, ranked only 46th in the world at the time, stormed to a personal-best time to claim the gold.

▼ Matt Biondi punches the air in delight as he wins the 50m freestyle race ahead of his American teammate and the world record holder in the event, Thomas Jager.

MEDAL TABLE	G	S	B
Soviet Union	55	31	46
East Germany	37	35	30
U.S.	36	31	27
South Korea	12	10	11
West Germany	11	14	15
Hungary	11	6	6
Bulgaria	10	12	13
Romania	7	11	6
France	6	4	6
Italy	6	4	4

ARCHERY, SHOOTING, AND FENCING

Three sports with ancient origins in war and combat, archery, shooting, and fencing demand ice-cold nerves and pinpoint precision. Archers and shooters repeat the same action over and over again, knowing that a slip of just a few millimeters could mean the end of their medal hopes. Champion fencers need accuracy and lightning-fast reactions, as well as the ability to predict an opponent's moves in a rapid, all-out battle of thrust and counter thrust.

◀ At the 1996 Olympics Dutch archer Ljudmila Arzhannikova takes aim and prepares to shoot. Competition archers wear a protective finger tab, as well as a chest guard that protects them from possible friction burns as the arrow flies away from the bow at speeds of more than 148 mph (240km/h).

▲ An archery target has ten rings. The closer to the center an arrow lands, the more points it scores. Hitting the smallest ring—the bull's-eye—scores ten.

Archery

Before 1920 archery was an Olympic event on a handful of occasions, but after that it was not seen again at the Games until 1972. Competitors shoot "ends" featuring a certain number of arrows, which must be shot within a time limit. In the ranking round, held before the Olympic competition, archers shoot 12 ends of six arrows each (a total of 72 arrows) in order to determine the best 64 archers. These archers then compete head-to-head in a series of elimination rounds. When only four archers are left, two semifinals and one final round determine the medal winners. At the Olympics individual events are held for both men and women. A team event for three archers was introduced to the Games in 1988.

Shooting

The 1900 Games featured live pigeon shooting, but at modern Olympics competitors aim at artificial targets. In the shotgun events shooters have to track and shoot "clay pigeons"—clay disks that are launched into the air from a device called a trap at speeds of around 62 mph (100km/h) and at different heights. Single and double trap events are held, as well as skeet shooting, in which two clay pigeons are launched, one on both sides of the shooter. Rifle and pistol shooters aim at paper targets that are either stationary or running (moving). Rifle shooters fire from three different positions: standing, kneeling, and lying on their stomachs (known as the prone position). The level of marksmanship on display at the Olympics is staggering. For example, at the 1996 Games Australian Michael Diamond competed in the men's trapshooting competition and hit an incredible 149 out of 150 targets, including 25 out of 25 in the final.

▶ Italian shooter and 1996 gold medalist Roberto di Donna prepares to fire a shot during the final of the men's 10m air pistol competition at the 2000 Games.

Fencing

This dynamic sport is one of only four to have featured in every modern Olympics. During a bout fencers wear protective clothing and masks and try to make scoring moves by striking their opponent's body. Team and individual events take place using three types of weapons: the foil, the saber, and the épée. The scoring rules for each weapon are different. With the foil, the scoring zone is limited to the opponent's torso; the saber scoring zone is the torso, arms, and head; and with the épée, all of the opponent's body, including the head, is a valid target. In contests that are often short but extremely tense fencers attack by lunging forward and defend by parrying (deflecting) their opponent's blows. The sport demands a cool head and a lot of experience, and champion fencers are often able to remain competitive for many years. Aladar Gerevich of Hungary, for example, won the team saber event in six consecutive Games between 1932 and 1960.

▲ Russian fencer Olga Charkova (left) and the U.S.'s Iris Zimmerman (right) compete in the women's individual foil event in Sydney in 2000. Fencers duel on a 46-ft. (14-m)-long and 5 -ft. (1.5-m)-wide playing zone called the piste. Their weapons are rigged with sensors that register each hit electronically.

▲ Wheelchair fencing is very popular in the Paralympics. Here Poland's Jadwiga Polasik (right) fights Hungary's Judit Palfi on her way to win gold in 2000. Poland won three out of the four women's fencing gold medals at the Games.

WEIGHT LIFTING, WRESTLING, AND BOXING

Fans of raw power flock to the Olympic weight-lifting, wrestling, and boxing arenas to see epic feats of strength performed by the competitors. These athletes train long and hard to build up imposing physiques, but each event also requires clever tactics and a great deal of technical skill. All three sports feature competitions at a range of different weight divisions.

Weight lifting

Great drama often surrounds Olympic weight-lifting competitions, where lifters must hoist into the air a set of weights that can be several times heavier than themselves—and keep them under control. Competitors announce their starting weight and have three attempts to lift each weight. There are two types of lifts at the Games: the two-stage clean and jerk (see diagram below) and the snatch, where the lift must be completed in one movement. In the combined event lifters perform both types, with their best effort in each category added together to produce a combined total weight. Female weight lifting debuted at the 2000 Games, with Chinese lifters winning gold in four of the seven weight divisions.

▲ *Naim Suleymanoglu, Turkish weight-lifting legend and winner of three Olympic gold medals, prepares for a lift at the 1996 Games. In 1988 the combined total for his two lifts was a staggering 342.5kg, yet he himself weighed less than 137 lbs. (62kg) (the upper limit for featherweight lifters).*

▼ *Russia's Aleksandr Karelin (in red) is considered to be the best super heavyweight Greco-Roman wrestler in Olympic history. Here he grapples with Siamak Ghaffari of the U.S. in 1996 on the way to his third gold medal in consecutive Games.*

▲ *The clean and jerk is a two-part lift. To begin, the lifter pulls the bar up toward her chest using the thigh and back muscles and then crouches to bring the bar under control. Stage two, the jerk, is performed by driving up with the legs and straightening the body. With feet together, the lifter must lock her arms, stay still, and have control of the bar in order for the lift to be legal.*

Wrestling

Two forms of this sport are found at the Olympics: freestyle and Greco-Roman. In both, bouts run for two rounds of three minutes each and take place within a yellow circle, which is 23 ft. (7m) in diameter. Wrestlers aim to pin their opponent by the shoulders to the mat. If the referee decides that the attacking wrestler has complete control, this is called a fall, and it wins the contest. Points are awarded for holds and throws, and a wrestler can also win by building a lead of ten points or by scoring more points than his rival by the end of the bout. In Greco-Roman wrestling the legs cannot be used in holds, and only holds above the hips are legal. Freestyle wrestling allows holds and grappling above and below the waist, and wrestlers can use their legs to push, trip, or lift.

Boxing

Olympic boxing is for amateur contestants who have qualified via regional tournaments held on each continent. The draw for bouts is made randomly, and each bout consists of four two-minute-long rounds. Points are scored when a boxer strikes his opponent on the side or the front of the body above the waist or on his head with the knuckle part of the glove. Punches made with other parts of the glove, those that strike the arms, or those that carry little force do not score. Three of the five judges must approve the punch in order for a point to be scored. A boxer whose hands or body hit the floor of the ring is considered knocked down and must submit to an eight-second count by the referee. The referee in the ring decides if the boxer can continue. A boxer who has not regained his balance after a count often is declared knocked out and loses the fight. Safety is paramount in Olympic boxing, and fouls and warnings for low blows and other dangerous moves can lead to disqualification. Since 1984 protective headgear has been worn, and boxers must be aged between 17 and 34. Doctors are present at the side of the ring, and they have the power to stop a bout for medical reasons.

◀ A young Cassius Clay stands proudly on the podium after receiving his gold medal in the light-heavyweight boxing event at the 1960 Rome Olympics. Clay turned professional shortly afterward, and in 1964 he changed his name to Muhammad Ali. Other Olympic gold medalists who went on to great professional success include Great Britain's Lennox Lewis and the U.S.'s George Foreman and Joe Frazier.

▲ Hungary's Laszlo Papp was the first boxer to win three Olympic gold medals in the middleweight and light-middleweight divisions (1948–1956). Papp later managed Hungary's national boxing team for 21 years.

▶ At the 2000 Games American Ricardo Williams Jr. (in red) throws a left-handed body punch while weaving to his right to avoid a punch from Nigeria's Olusegun Ajose. Williams went on to win silver in the light-welterweight division.

JUDO AND TAE KWON DO

The Olympics' two martial arts first appeared in the Games as temporary or demonstration sports (judo in the 1964 Tokyo Games and tae kwon do in Seoul in 1988). Today they have full-medal status. Champion judo and tae kwon do competitors require balance, poise, strength, and explosive reactions. They also need mental agility and great strength in order to counter every move of their opponents in a fascinating head-to-head contest.

▲ *David Douillet of France beats Japan's Shinichi Shinohara to win the heavyweight judo gold medal at the Sydney Olympics. Douillet also won gold at the 1996 Games and bronze in 1992.*

46 ft. (14m)
Safety zone

20 ft. (6m)
Contest area

3 ft. (1m)
Danger zone

Starting positions

◀ *Judo bouts are held on foam mats. The action occurs in the central contest area, which is surrounded by a red strip called the danger zone. The outer safety zone is out-of-bounds to competitors.*

Judo

The word "judo" is Japanese for "the gentle way." Developed in the late 1800s, it is a form of unarmed self-defense and combat in which two competitors, known as judoka, try to use the momentum of their opponent to unbalance him or her. Under the close eye of a referee and a series of judges, a judoka scores points by executing throws and holds and by pinning the opponent to the mat. Japan is the dominant judo nation, but the sport's growing worldwide popularity has seen Olympic medal winners from a wide range of nations, including South Korea, Russia, Georgia, France, the Netherlands, and Cuba.

▶ *Belgium's Nicole Flagothier is thrown by Great Britain's Nicola Fairbrother at the 1992 Games. Fairbrother went on to win silver in the lightweight division.*

▲ *Caught from behind, the judoka in white performs a sweeping hip throw called harai-goshi—one of the most common judo throws.*

▲ *Gripping her opponent by the waist, the attacking judoka throws her right leg back to sweep the opponent up onto her hip.*

▲ *Using her arms to complete the throw, the judoka in white throws her opponent to the floor, where she lands on her back.*

Ippon and waza-ari

A judo bout ends immediately if a judoka manages to score a key point called an ippon. This is obtained by executing one of a range of throws. The opponent must land mainly on his or her back, and the throw must be made with almost perfect standards of force, control, and speed. Ippon can also be scored by pinning the opponent to the mat for 25 seconds or if the opponent gives in by tapping the mat twice while being held. Waza-ari is worth half an ippon and is scored if a hold is maintained for 20 seconds or if a throw is made that satisfies almost all of the criteria of the judges. Two waza-ari awarded to the same contestant means that they win the bout. If a bout is not ended in this way, the judoka with the most points at the end of four minutes (in women's judo) or five minutes (in men's) is the winner.

▲ Great Britain's Darren Kail grapples with Sergiy Sydorenko of the Ukraine in the men's 66kg blind judo competition at the 2000 Paralympics. The rules are almost identical to regular judo, except that the judoka start their bout at arm's length apart.

Tae kwon do

Despite its origins in centuries'-old martial art traditions, tae kwon do was only formalized as a sport in the second half of the 1900s. It became an Olympic medal event in 2000, and this new arrival to the Games offers a fascinating blend of grace and agility on one hand and explosive power on the other. The force of the kicks and blows performed by the two opponents is so great that all competitors must wear extensive protection, including a helmet, a padded trunk protector, and shin, groin, and forearm guards.

▼ Australia's Paul Lyons launches into a spectacular two-footed kick during the Sydney Games. Lyons competed in the lightest of the four weight divisions found in men's tae kwon do. The women's competition is also divided into four weight classes. Both men and women wear a uniform of a white jacket and pants, called a dobok.

Points and penalties

Tae kwon do is a lightning-fast sport in which competitors seek to execute an array of blows (mainly kicks) while blocking or avoiding their opponent's attacks and staying balanced. The goal is either to knock out the opponent or to score more points than him or her during the full contest. Points are awarded by three judges, while a referee controls the contest on a mat measuring 39 ft. x 39 ft. (12m x 12m). A bout is held over three rounds, each three minutes long, and points are scored for landing a technically correct blow on one of the scoring areas—the head, the abdomen, and the sides of the body. Points are deducted for a range of offenses. These are divided into kyong-go (half-point or warning) penalties for offenses such as feigning injury or holding the opponent and gam-jeom (full-point) penalties for offenses such as throwing the opponent. If a competitor picks up a third penalty point, they lose the bout immediately.

GYMNASTICS

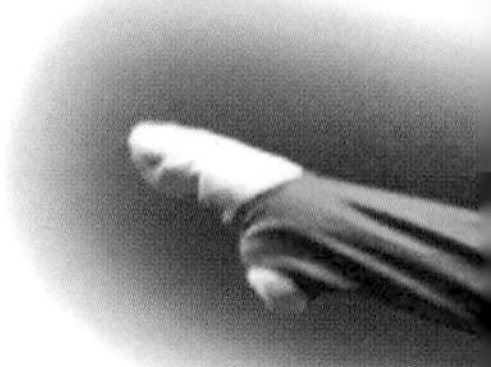

Gymnastics, in various forms, has been a breathtaking and very popular Olympic sport throughout the modern era. A Summer Games without the grace, strength, and magnificent agility of its gymnasts is simply unthinkable. Gymnastics today is split into artistic gymnastics, rhythmic gymnastics—which made its debut at the Los Angeles Games in 1984—and trampolining, the sport's newest Olympic event.

◀ Rhythmic gymnast Yulia Raskina of Belarus performs with the ribbon apparatus. Raskina scored 39.548 out of a possible 40 to win silver in the individual event behind Russia's Yulia Barsukova, who scored a remarkable 39.632 points.

▶ Trampolining made its Olympic debut in Sydney. Here Irina Karavaeva of Russia performs a high-flying move during the women's final, in which the eight best contestants from the qualifying round compete. Karavaeva went on to win the gold medal. Her teammate, Alexander Moskalenko, won gold in the men's event.

OLYMPIC LEGEND

Olga Korbut (born 1955)

Nationality: *Russian*
Games: *Munich 1972, Montreal 1976*
Event: *artistic gymnastics*
Medals: *four gold, two silver*

Rhythmic gymnastics and trampolining

Rhythmic gymnastics, which is only for women, features both team and individual events. Competitors perform routines on a square floor area that measures 43 ft. x 43 ft. (13m x 13m) using five different pieces of apparatus: rope, ball, clubs, ribbon, and hoop. Routines are choreographed to music, must be between 75 and 90 seconds long, and use the entire floor area while the apparatus is in constant motion. Three panels of judges award marks on technical merit, execution, and artistic merit. The trampolining competition begins with a qualifying round of two routines—one compulsory and one original. Marks are awarded for style and the execution of moves in both routines. The best competitors go through to the final, where they perform a single, original routine. Routines have no time limits, but competitors must show ten recognized skills, including landing on their back and front and performing a forward somersault with a twist. Trampolinists try to work spectacular moves into their routines such as the triff—a triple somersault with a twist—and the Randolph—a forward somersault with two-and-a-half twists.

Artistic gymnastics

In the hugely popular Olympic sport of artistic gymnastics competitors perform moves or routines on a range of apparatus. Medals are awarded to the best individual gymnasts on each apparatus: balance beam, vault, uneven bars, and floor exercises for women and horizontal bar, parallel bars, rings, pommel horse, vault, and floor exercises for men. There are also team events and medals for the best all-around individuals, whose marks are taken from performances on all of the apparatus. Two judges award each routine a mark out of ten for the degree of difficulty, while a second panel of six judges gives marks out of ten for execution. Points are removed for errors. For example, falling off a piece of apparatus costs a gymnast 0.5 points, while a small error in positioning can mean a loss of 0.1 points. The highest and lowest marks for execution are discarded, and the other four are averaged to determine the final score.

◀ The Ukraine's Oleksandr Beresh performs a swinging move on the parallel bars during the men's team event in Sydney. His team won silver behind China. At the end of a parallel bars routine the gymnast dismounts and lands beside the apparatus.

▼ Romanian Nadia Comaneci, shown here on the balance beam, amazed spectators at the 1976 Montreal Games with flawless performances on a number of apparatus. She became the first gymnast to score a perfect ten from the judges at the Olympics.

▶ In the vaulting competition gymnasts, such as the U.S.'s Blaine Wilson (pictured), approach the vaulting horse at full speed. Jumping off of a springboard, they place both hands on top of the horse and then perform one or a series of acrobatic turns in the air before landing.

Grace under pressure

Gymnastics has been an important part of the Olympics for more than 100 years, but in the 1970s the sport received a major boost to its popularity thanks to two gymnasts in particular. The Soviet Union's Olga Korbut produced performances of great style and originality, while Romanian Nadia Comaneci's flawless technical displays were simply breathtaking. The grace and poise on show in artistic gymnastics often disguise the immense strength required to hold a position perfectly on the rings or in the floor exercises or to explode off a vaulting horse in order to perform a spectacular vault. But gymnasts need much, much more than strength—incredible flexibility, perfect timing, artistic flair, and original routines, for example. In all apparatus events landing with perfect balance and without taking any extra steps—known as "sticking the landing"—is vital.

◀ Elena Zamolodtchikova of Russia performs her floor routine during the Sydney Games. In the women's event the floor routine is set to music. Gymnasts must interpret the music with grace and must also perform a series of moves. These include spectacular acts of tumbling, featuring somersaults and twists.

BARCELONA 1992

Barcelona had a long wait to be awarded its first Olympics. The Spanish city had originally been promised the 1924 Games before a last-minute decision switched the location to Paris. In 1992 Barcelona proved itself to be an exciting and successful host city for the first Olympics in 20 years not to be affected by boycotts. The Games are remembered for a series of exciting competitions, spectacular opening and closing ceremonies, fairly few controversies, and many notable firsts.

▲ *The official emblem of the Barcelona Games featured a colorful symbol—representing an athlete jumping over an obstacle formed by the Olympic rings.*

Paralympic success

The 1988 Seoul Games were the first in which Paralympians had access to major Olympic facilities and competed in the same venues as those used by Olympians. With the support of more than 8,000 volunteers, the success of the Seoul Paralympics was bolstered in Barcelona. More than 3,000 athletes from 82 nations took part, creating 279 new world records in the process. Their feats were watched by a live audience of around 1.5 million people—cementing the future of the Paralympics as a major sports spectacle.

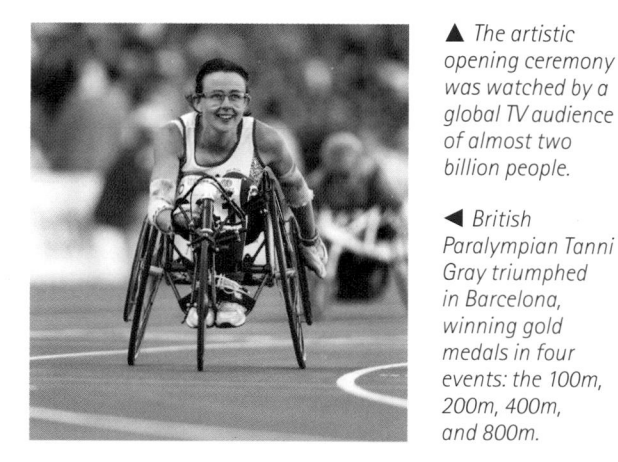

▲ *The artistic opening ceremony was watched by a global TV audience of almost two billion people.*

◀ *British Paralympian Tanni Gray triumphed in Barcelona, winning gold medals in four events: the 100m, 200m, 400m, and 800m.*

Welcome to all nations

A record 9,367 competitors from 169 nations made Barcelona the largest Summer Games up to that point. The end of the apartheid system of racial segregation in South Africa saw that country welcomed back to the Olympic movement after a 32-year break. The Soviet Union was in the process of dissolving into a number of separate republics, and their athletes appeared under the title of the Commonwealth of Independent States, also known as the Unified Team (UT). Namibia, Croatia, and Slovenia all made their Olympic debuts, while a unified German team competed for the first time since 1936, winning an impressive 33 golds. In men's field hockey Andreas Keller became the third generation of his family to represent Germany and to win an Olympic medal in that sport.

◀ *The U.S's basketball team, made up of superstars from the professional NBA (National Basketball Association) league, was nicknamed the "Dream Team." On its way to winning the gold medal the team scored more than 100 points in every game. Here Michael Jordan (9) reaches for a rebound surrounded by teammates (left to right) Larry Bird, Magic Johnson, and Scottie Pippen.*

▶ *Vitaly Scherbo demonstrates perfect posture in the crucifix move as he takes part in the rings competition. Scherbo, of the Unified Team, won this event and a further five gymnastics competitions to become the leading individual medal winner of the Barcelona Games.*

MEDAL TABLE	G	S	B
Unified Team	45	38	29
U.S.	37	34	37
Germany	33	21	28
China	16	22	16
Cuba	14	6	11
Spain	13	7	2
South Korea	12	5	12
Hungary	11	12	7
France	8	5	16
Australia	7	9	11

Dreams and few nightmares

Fearing terrorism, the Spanish government spent an estimated $400 million on security at the Games. There were no major incidents, but there was plenty of drama in the events. Great Britain's Linford Christie became the oldest-ever winner of the men's 100m, while favorite Sergei Bubka failed to clear a single pole vault. Badminton made its Olympic debut, with South Korea and Indonesia sweeping the gold medals, while women's judo and men's baseball also made their first appearances.

A change in the basketball rules admitted professional players for the first time, and the U.S.'s "Dream Team" dominated the 1992 Games, winning their matches by a huge average of 43.2 points and even beating silver medalists Croatia by a substantial 32-point margin.

▶ *One of the most memorable scenes from Barcelona featured British 400m runner Derek Redmond, who injured his hamstring in the semifinal. In agony, he insisted on completing the race, limping around the track supported by his father.*

On the water

Yachting and rowing were a big success in Barcelona. Prince Felipe, the son of Spain's King Juan Carlos, competed in a solo yachting event but did not win a medal. The coxed eights rowing final saw the smallest-ever winning margin of less than one inch, as Canada edged ahead of Romania for the gold. In the same event Carlos Front, the cox of the Spanish boat, became the youngest Olympic competitor since 1896. He was only 11 years old.

▶ *In the 10,000m Ethiopia's Derartu Tulu (left) became the first female black African to win Olympic gold. Elana Meyer (right) of South Africa won silver.*

▲ *The German women's field hockey team defend a short corner in the Barcelona Games. The team reached the final, where they were beaten by Spain. The German men's team went one step farther, beating Australia to win team gold.*

CYCLING

Cycling, in many different forms, has been part of the Olympics since the first Games in 1896. Some events, such as the 2,000m tandem race, have fallen by the wayside, while new races, such as the keirin, have been added. In the early 1990s professional cyclists, who practice and perform at the Tour de France and other races, were allowed to compete in the Games, adding glamour and star names to an already very popular Olympic spectacle.

▲ The women's road race in Sydney begins with a group start. Road racing features lightweight, geared bikes that look more like regular bicycles than the super-streamlined track machines.

◄ France's Miguel Martinez negotiates a tricky downhill part of the Sydney Olympic mountain biking course on his way to win gold in the men's cross-country. Good balance, control, and great stamina are vital in this grueling sport.

Mountain biking

Cycling is divided into road, track, and mountain-biking events. Mountain biking is the newest addition and calls for great strength and skill in negotiating the tough terrain of a cross-country course. The race is designed to last around two hours and 15 minutes and is held over a number of laps of a twisting course featuring sharp hills, gullies, and treacherous descents. This amounts to between 40 and 50km for men and from 30 to 40km for women. The terrain is so tricky that, in places, some riders choose to dismount and carry their bikes. Others gamble on managing to stay on their machines in the hope of gaining time on their rivals. Collisions and punctures do occur, so competitors carry small toolboxes on their bikes just in case.

► Great Britain passes Russia to win the team pursuit quarterfinal at the Sydney velodrome. The bikes have no brakes and are built from lightweight materials such as titanium and carbon fiber.

On the road

There are two Olympic road-racing events held over different distances at each Games: the individual time trial (around 50km for men and 30km for women) and the individual road race (around 220km for men and 110km for women). The time trial is a race against the clock, with riders setting off at 90-second intervals, striving to complete the course in the fastest time in order to win gold. In the road race an individual is crowned champion, but teamwork often features. Cyclists from one nation look after their best rider by allowing him or her to ride in their slipstream in order to stay fresh for a sprint finish. Road racing is a supreme test of fitness, which makes Jeannie Longo-Ciprelli's feat of competing in five Olympics even more remarkable. Her bronze medal in Sydney came at the age of 41.

◄ Dutch cyclist Leontien Zijlaard competes in the women's individual pursuit in 2000, an event that she eventually won. Her bike has spokeless wheels and she grips forward-facing handlebars, called aerobars, in order to create as streamlined a racing position as possible.

In the velodrome

Most Olympic cycling events are held on the steeply sloped track of a velodrome. Track races are divided into sprints (between 500m and 2,000m) and endurance events (up to 60km). In the individual pursuit two riders start at the halfway points of the two opposing straights of the track and aim to complete the 4,000m (for men) or 3,000m (for women) in a quicker time than their opponent. The four-person team pursuit is similar. Each team's time is measured at the point that the third cyclist crosses the finish line. This event can be won earlier if a team catches up with and passes the opposition. The 1,000m time trial is a flat-out sprint, with riders accelerating as quickly as possible from a standing start. One of the most exciting events is the keirin, in which riders are paced by a motorized vehicle called a derny for the first 1,400m of the 2,000m race. After 1,400m—and with the pace already high—the cyclists begin a spectacular sprint for the finish line.

OLYMPIC LEGEND
Jeannie Longo-Ciprelli (born 1958)

Nationality: *French*
Games: *Los Angeles 1984, Seoul 1988, Barcelona 1992, Atlanta 1996, Sydney 2000*
Events: *time trial, road race*
Medals: *one gold, two silver, one bronze*

61

EQUESTRIAN EVENTS

More than 2,600 years ago four-horse chariot racing was one of the most spectacular and dangerous events at the ancient Olympics. The modern equestrian program of jumping, dressage, and eventing was introduced at the 1912 Games. These events have remained in the Olympics ever since, despite a crisis in 1956 when the Australian quarantine laws would not allow foreign horses to enter the country, and the equestrian events had to be staged in Stockholm, Sweden.

◄ *Equestrianism is one of the few Olympic sports that features men and women competing on the same teams or against each other. Here Margie Goldstein of the U.S., riding a horse named Perrin, jumps over a rail fence during the individual qualifying jumping round at the Sydney Games.*

Jumping

In Olympic jumping riders and horses must work together extremely well in order to clear a course featuring between 15 and 20 jump obstacles. These include water jumps, parallel rails, and combination obstacles made up of two or three fences placed one after another.

The goal is to complete the course without picking up penalties, which are known as faults. These are incurred if a horse knocks down part of an obstacle, refuses to jump over an obstacle at the first attempt, puts a foot in the water at a water jump, or makes the jumps in the wrong order. If there is a tie for first place, then the course is altered, and a jump-off against the clock takes place. The winner is the rider with the fewest faults. In the event of another tie the rider with the fastest time wins gold.

Dressage

Sometimes described as ballet for horses, dressage has its origins in a method of training horses in the military. Rider and horse must work in perfect harmony to perform a series of complicated moves, such as the figure eight, at three different speeds: walk, trot, and canter. A panel of five judges assesses the performance of each rider and horse, marking every move they perform. The rider must appear to be sitting perfectly still and upright at all times, yet the horse must respond to instructions made by the rider in the form of slight movements. Riders cannot speak or make sounds to their horse, and whips are not allowed. Four riders compete in the team event, with the scores of the best three riders added together to form their team total. The final round of the individual event is freestyle, in which riders perform their own routine set to music.

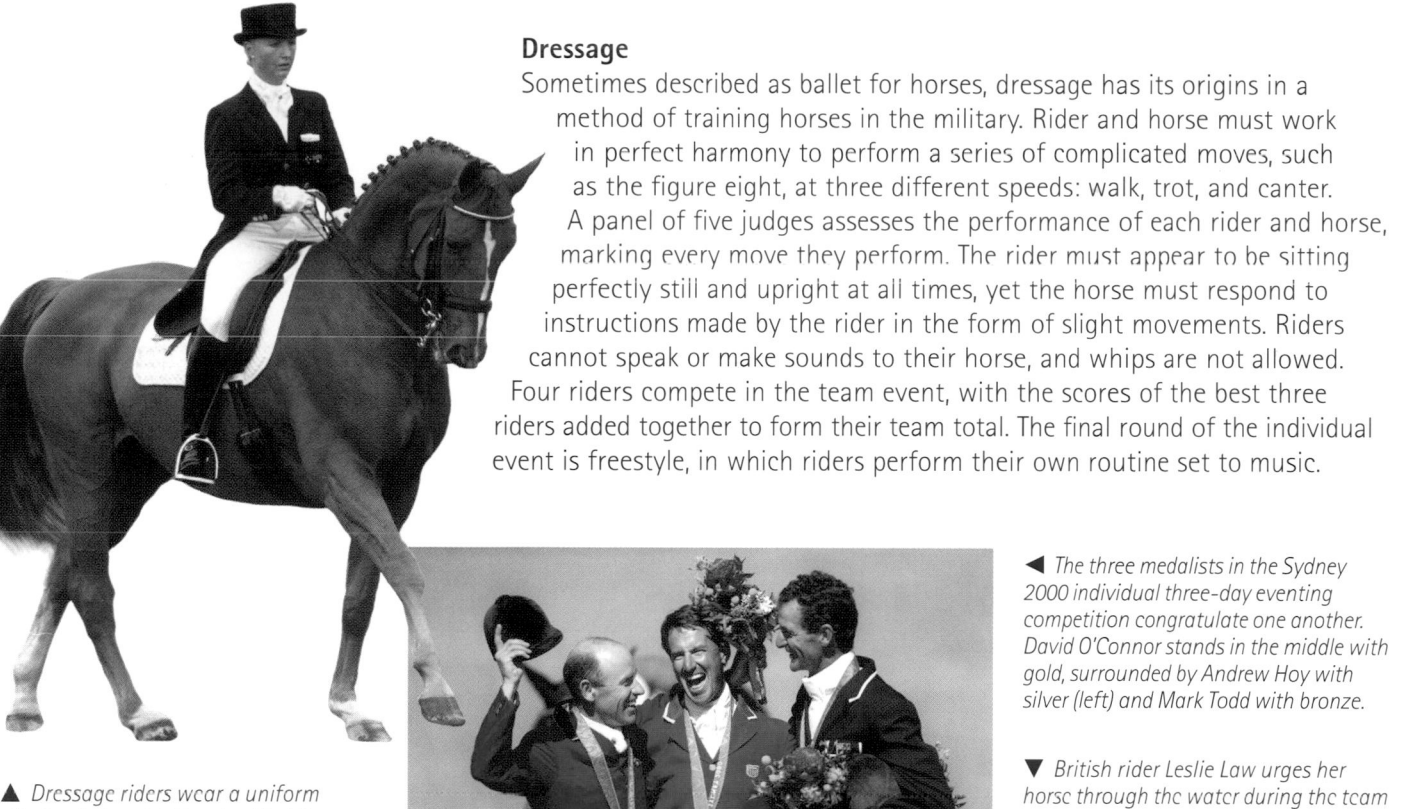

◀ The three medalists in the Sydney 2000 individual three-day eventing competition congratulate one another. David O'Connor stands in the middle with gold, surrounded by Andrew Hoy with silver (left) and Mark Todd with bronze.

▲ Dressage riders wear a uniform of a top hat and tailcoat with riding breeches (pants). Here Australia's Kristy Oatley-Nist competes in the individual dressage at the Sydney Games in 2000.

▼ British rider Leslie Law urges her horse through the water during the team eventing endurance test in Sydney. Law was a member of the four-person British team that won silver in this event.

Eventing

Equestrian eventing takes place over three days. In both the individual and team competitions horses and riders perform a dressage test and complete a jumping course over fences. Sandwiched between these is the toughest test of all, the endurance discipline. Held over a cross-country course around 15.5 mi. (25km) in length, the endurance test features several different challenges, including a steeplechase, in which three fences must be jumped three times each, and an obstacle section, in which horse and rider must negotiate tricky drops, ditches, banks, and water jumps. In addition, there is a jumping course of fences—usually set lower than the official jumping fences—to encounter at the end of this grueling day. At all stages riders try to complete the various sections of the course within time limits and without incurring faults from falls, refusals, or other penalties.

▶ Australia's Gillian Rolton falls from her horse, Peppermint Grove, during the team eventing competition at the 1996 Atlanta Games. Despite breaking her collarbone and two ribs, Rolton remounted and completed the course. Her Australian team went on to win the gold medal.

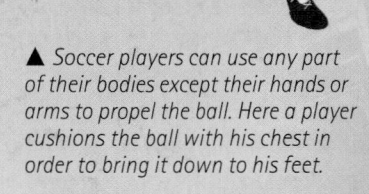

TEAM BALL SPORTS 2

Soccer, volleyball, and handball are fast-moving team sports that attract big Olympic crowds. Soccer was first played at the Games in 1900, while volleyball debuted in Tokyo in 1964. Handball was an 11-on-11 outdoor sport in 1936, but it returned to the Olympics in 1972 as an indoor seven-on-seven game. Beach volleyball is the newest arrival, introduced as an Olympic event in 1996.

▲ Soccer players can use any part of their bodies except their hands or arms to propel the ball. Here a player cushions the ball with his chest in order to bring it down to his feet.

Soccer

Soccer is the most popular team ball sport in the world, widely played and watched by both men and women. It is an 11-on-11 game, with teams striving to score more goals than the opposition over two halves of 45 minutes each. Soccer is definitely a favorite event at the Olympics—in 1956, for example, in the Australian city of Melbourne, a first-round game between Sweden and Brazil attracted a crowd of 93,000 people. When the Olympic tournament reaches the quarter-final stage, games that end in a tie result in a period of extra time being played. If the teams are still tied after extra time, the game climaxes in a tense and exciting penalty shoot-out.

◄ The Norwegian women's soccer team pose with their winner's medals in 2000. With the final against the U.S. tied at 2-2, the game went into extra time. Norway scored a third goal to win gold.

▼ The Cameroon men's team celebrate moments after winning gold at the Sydney Games by beating Spain in a penalty shoot-out.

▼ The goalkeeper is the one player in soccer who is allowed to handle the ball on the field. This can only be done inside the goalkeeper's own penalty area.

From amateur to professional

Until the emergence of the World Cup in the 1930s the Olympics were the stage for the biggest international soccer championship in the world. Traditionally, only amateur soccer players were allowed to take part in the Games, but since the 1980s professional players—with some age restrictions—have been permitted. Sydney 2000 saw well-known professionals, such as Brazil's Ronaldinhio, Cameroon's Lauren, and Japan's Hidetoshi Nakata, take part in a tournament that produced an average of more than three goals per game. The biggest change to Olympic soccer came in the 1990s with the arrival of the women's competition, which was first won by the U.S. in 1996. Ten women's teams and 16 men's teams will compete for the gold medal at the 2004 Athens Games.

Volleyball

Both indoor volleyball and beach volleyball are played on a 59-ft. (18-m)-long, 30-ft. (9-m)-wide court with a net raised to a height of 8 ft. (2.43m) for men and 7.3 ft. (2.24m) for women. Indoor volleyball involves six players working together to keep the ball airborne and inside the court. Each team is allowed no more than three touches before the ball has to travel over the net to the opposition's side. A player can use any part of his or her body to hit the ball but must then wait for the ball to be touched by another player before hitting it again. Beach volleyball is played on level sand, with most of the same rules and a ball of the same size—although this is inflated to a greater pressure, making it heavier and more stable in the wind. With just two players per side, competitors need to cover large amounts of ground and work closely together. A weaker player in a team is quickly exploited by the opposition.

▼ Australia's Kerri Pottharst dives to reach the ball in the final of the women's beach volleyball competition in Sydney. Pottharst and her teammate, Natalie Cook, beat the Brazilian favorites in the final to add gold to the bronze medal they collected four years earlier.

Handball

The rules of handball lead to a fast and free-flowing game, with most of the action concentrated around the goal areas. Particularly popular in eastern Europe, at the Olympics handball is a seven-on-seven sport played on a court that is 131 ft. (40m) long and 66 ft. (20m) wide. Players pass, throw, and catch a small ball, with the goal of launching it past the opposition's goalkeeper and into the net. An arc, 20 ft. (6m) from the goal, forms the D-shaped goal area, in which the keeper is the only player who can be involved in active play. The keeper is also the only player who is allowed to use his or her feet and legs below the knee to stop the ball from heading toward the goal. When a player catches the ball, he or she is allowed to take three steps and hold onto the ball for three seconds before passing it. Players can also dribble it like a basketball and roll it along the floor. Just like in basketball, rolling substitutions (see p. 64) are allowed.

▶ Spain's Rafael Pascual has a shot blocked by Reinder Nummerdor of the Netherlands during the men's indoor volleyball competition in Sydney. The Dutch side went on to win the game by three sets to one (25–18, 25–17, 24–26, 25–21).

◀ Denmark, the women's handball champions at the 1996 Olympics, pose for a photo after winning gold again in 2000. The Danish team managed to claw back from a six-point deficit to beat Hungary 31–27 in the final, with Anette Hoffman Moberg scoring 11 goals.

◀ Brazil's Viviani Emerick leaps into the air to launch a shot on the goal during the Sydney Games. The ball in women's handball measures 21–22 in. (54–56cm) in diameter. In the men's event it is slightly larger, with a diameter of 23–24 in. (58–60cm).

RACKET SPORTS

Tennis is one of the most popular and widely played ball sports in the world, and its return to the Olympics in 1988 delighted millions of fans. Table tennis and badminton are also fairly new arrivals to the Games (debuting in 1988 and 1992), but both come with a huge and dedicated following of players and spectators, particularly from Europe and Asia.

▲ Great Britain takes on China in a badminton doubles match at the 2000 Olympics. China had staggering success in Sydney, with their three women's pairs each winning a medal and the badminton team as a whole collecting eight of the 15 medals available.

Badminton

Originally popular as a sport among the wealthy in the late 1800s, badminton is today the world's fastest racket sport, so competitors have to be excellent athletes. The game involves individuals or pairs of players using lightweight rackets to hit a nylon or feather shuttlecock across a net into the opposition's side of the court. Points are scored when the serving player forces his or her opponent into making a mistake—knocking the shuttlecock into the net or out of the court, for example—or if they manage to get the shuttlecock to hit the floor on their opponent's side. Matches are contested over the best of three games, and players require great agility and quick reactions to attack and defend because the shuttlecock reaches speeds of up to 161 mph (260km/h).

▶ During a men's badminton doubles match South Korea's Yoo Yong-Sung jumps into the air to time a powerful overhead smash. Along with his partner, Lee Dong-Soo, he won a silver medal in this competition at the 2000 Games.

Table tennis

Millions of people have enjoyed a casual game of Ping-Pong™, but that is a world away from table tennis at the Olympics. Recent changes to the scoring and serving rules have encouraged full-blown attacking play, with competitors capable of hitting the ball at speeds of up to 99 mph (160km/h). Matches in the Olympic table tennis finals are the best of seven games. To win a game, a player must score 11 points or, if both players are tied at ten, to move ahead by two clear points. Table tennis is not just a spectacular power sport, but it is also a game of accuracy, speed, and tactics. Table tennis champions can hit the ball with a wide variety of shots, imparting a spin on the ball so that it changes its trajectory in midair and as it bounces. Sidespin shots make the ball swerve dramatically in the air, while powerful topspin shots see the ball loop up, bounce, and accelerate off the opponent's side of the table.

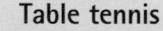

▶ In this table tennis match at Sydney 2000 the attacking player throws his whole body into a spectacular forehand smash. Although he strikes the ball with great force, he must time and position the shot with pinpoint accuracy in order to land the ball on the opponent's half of the table. Each player's side measures only 4.5 ft. (1.37m) long by 5 ft. (1.525m) wide.

◀ This defending table tennis player has to employ lightning-fast reactions in order to respond to the powerful attacking shot of his opponent. Backspin is often applied to defensive shots to make the ball lose speed after it bounces.

▶ Russia's Yevgeny Kafelnikov powers through a serve during the men's singles tennis competition at the Sydney Games. Serving is a potent weapon in men's tennis, with servers trying to send the ball over to their opponent at great speed or with placement and spin, making it very difficult or impossible to return. A serve that the opposing player is unable to touch with his or her racket is called an ace.

Tennis

In Seoul in 1988 tennis was welcomed back into the Olympics after a 64-year absence and with professional players allowed to compete. Tennis at the Games, just like at Wimbledon and other major tournaments, is a knockout competition with singles and doubles events for men and women. For both sexes each match is played as the best of three sets, except for the men's final, which is the best of five sets. Players who lose in the semifinals compete in a play-off for third place and a bronze medal. Top tennis players must be able to anticipate their opponent's shots, cover the court quickly, and have a strong, accurate serve that does not weaken under pressure. Some players prefer to stay at the back, or baseline, of the court, hitting ground strokes and engaging in long rallies. Others like to come up to the net, attacking with volleys and powerful smash shots.

▶ American tennis star Venus Williams keeps her eye on the ball as she winds up to play a two-handed backhand shot. Williams claimed two gold medals at the Sydney Olympics, beating Russia's Yelena Dementyeva in the singles and winning the women's doubles with her sister Serena.

SYDNEY 2000

On September 15, 2000 the greatest show on Earth came to Australia for the second time. The 1956 Melbourne Olympics had been a happy, peaceful, but fairly low-key affair. The Sydney Olympics took the Games to a completely different level. Sixteen days later, after dozens of memorable scenes and incredible performances, the president of the IOC, Juan Antonio Samaranch, declared the Sydney Games the best ever. Few disagreed.

▲ The official symbol of the 2000 Summer Olympics, the largest Games ever, with 10,651 athletes from 199 nations competing in 300 different events. Thirty-six venues, including the gigantic stadium in Homebush Bay, were used.

▼ Cathy Freeman captivated her home crowd and the world with a 400m victory under extreme pressure. As a symbol of Australia's aborigines, Freeman had been the bearer of the Olympic torch at the opening ceremony of the Games.

Huge public support

Sydney's success was largely due to the Australian people, who volunteered in their thousands and flocked to the events, snapping up many of the five million tickets on sale. Australia's athletes responded with their best-ever Olympic performance, scooping 58 medals. The Australians were praised for their passionate yet fair support for all the competitors. In the men's long jump, for example, the home crowd gave enthusiastic support to Cuba's Ivan Pedroso, even after he had beaten Australia's Jai Taurima to the gold.

▲ Steve Redgrave celebrates the fifth Olympic gold of his career, won as part of the British coxless fours rowing team that beat crews from Australia and Italy.

◀ *Ian Thorpe, nicknamed the "Thorpedo," powers his way to gold and a new world record in the 400m freestyle competition. Thorpe won a total of three golds and two silvers in Sydney's state-of-the-art Aquatic Center.*

Stand-out performances

Shocks, surprises, and amazing stories abounded throughout the Sydney Olympics. Cycling legend Lance Armstrong was expected to win in the 50km cycling time trial but lost to his close friend, Russian Vyacheslav Ekimov. Another Russian, Aleksandr Karelin, lost his 13-year-long unbeaten record in Greco-Roman wrestling to American Rulon Gardner. Two German female athletes, the long jumper Heike Drechsler and the kayaker Birgit Fischer, turned back time and won gold medals, beating much younger opponents. For Fischer there was a 20-year gap between her two kayaking golds. Swimming stars at the Games included Ian Thorpe of Australia and the Netherlands' Inge de Bruijn, who won three golds and a silver.

MEDAL TABLE	G	S	B
U.S.	39	25	33
Russia	32	28	28
China	28	16	15
Australia	16	25	17
Germany	14	17	26
France	13	14	11
Italy	13	8	13
Netherlands	12	9	4
Cuba	11	11	7
Great Britain	11	10	7

▶ *Annet Davis of the U.S. and Australia's Sarah Stratton challenge a point in the women's beach volleyball competition, held on Sydney's world-famous Bondi Beach.*

◀ *The spectacular closing ceremony, held at the Sydney stadium on October 1, 2000, entertained 110,000 enthralled spectators.*

Noteworthy firsts

British rower Steve Redgrave won his fifth gold in as many Olympics, a feat never achieved before in an endurance sport. Colombia celebrated its first-ever gold medal when 35-year-old Maria Isabel Urrutia won a women's weightlifting gold. This was a double first since women's weighlifting also made its first appearance at the Sydney Games. Synchronized diving, women's pole-vaulting, the triathlon, and tae kwon do also made their Olympic debuts, with the latter event seeing South Korean champion Kim Kyong-Hun win heavyweight gold and Greece and China also win medals in this martial art.

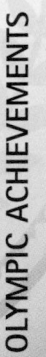

GREAT RIVALRIES

The history of the Olympics, like all great sports occasions, is marked with compelling tales of great rivalries between talented athletes or between teams and nations. From time to time intense contests can lead to clashes, but more often these rivalries are kept under control and only help propel Olympians to greater levels of performance and achievement.

▼ The rivalry between long-distance runners Haile Gebrselassie (left) and Paul Tergat (right) has produced some of the most exciting races and nail-biting finishes in the history of the sport. Of the two, Gebrselassie has always been the athlete to win Olympic gold, narrowly beating his rival into the silver medal position on two occasions.

▲ British athlete Daley Thompson (left) and West German Jürgen Hingsen (right) pushed themselves to new heights in the decathlon as they battled each other for the top spot. Thompson won gold in 1980 and 1984.

Dueling decathletes

In the late 1970s and 1980s the decathlon was dominated by British athlete Daley Thompson and a trio from West Germany—Guido Kratschmer, Siggy Wentz, and Jürgen Hingsen. Thompson and Hingsen formed an especially fierce rivalry, trading world records in decathlons all around the world. After winning gold at the 1980 Games Thompson faced a severe test at the Los Angeles Olympics, especially because Hingsen had just broken Thompson's world record. Both men repeatedly set new personal bests and broke Olympic records in the course of the competition before Thompson finally triumphed. Thompson's points tally was later upgraded to a new world record. "Some day I'll beat him. Of course, I may be 80 by then," Hingsen joked afterward. The rivalry continued through to a third Olympics in 1988, but injury for Thompson and Hingsen's disqualification from the 100m for false starts meant that neither man reached the heights of their previous meetings.

Smiling rivals

Ethiopia versus Kenya, Haile Gebrselassie versus Paul Tergat. One of the world's great track-and-field rivalries has been fought over long-distance races, including the 5,000m, cross-country, and marathon competitions. Two of their most famous meetings were at the Olympics, both in the 10,000m. At the 1996 Games Gebrselassie beat Tergat by only a few meters. Tergat overtook Gebrselassie's 10,000m world record in 1997 and also beat him in a number of other events. But Gebrselassie was the favorite as the pair renewed their intense but friendly rivalry in Sydney in 2000. In a dramatic race Tergat was ahead until the last stride. After more than 27 minutes of racing only nine hundredths of a second separated Gebrselassie's first place from Tergat's second. Their enthusiastic rivalry had produced the most exciting long-distance race finish in Olympic history.

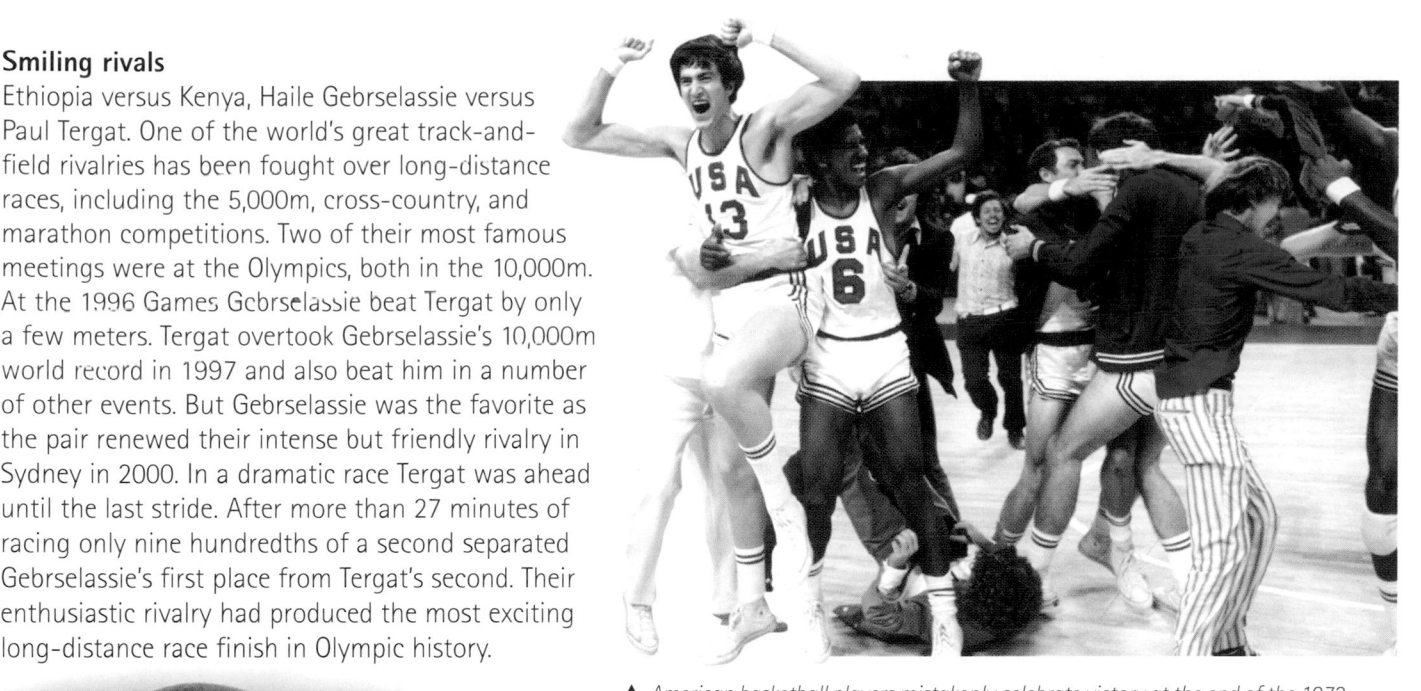

▲ American basketball players mistakenly celebrate victory at the end of the 1972 final. In fact, the game was not over, and their bitter rivals, the Soviet Union, snatched victory in the last seconds. The Americans' silver medals remain uncollected in a safe at the IOC headquarters.

Team rivalries

Great rivalries are not always restricted to two individual athletes. There is an intense and long-standing rivalry, for example, between the boxers of Cuba and the U.S., the field hockey players of India and Pakistan, and the weight-lifting teams of Greece, Turkey, and Bulgaria. One of the most intense of all team rivalries occurs in the pool between the powerhouse swimming nations of the U.S. and Australia. Going back to the 1920s, when American swimmer Johnny Weissmuller dominated many events, the rivalry has seen these two nations finish first and second in the Olympic swimming medal table an astonishing nine times.

Going too far

Sometimes a rivalry breaks out into open hostility or a refusal to accept defeat. In 1996 after an epic women's volleyball semifinal ended with Cuba beating Brazil the players started pushing and shoving each other. Neither team was disqualified, and Cuba went on to win gold. During the height of the Cold War the sporting rivalry between the U.S. and the Soviet Union escalated, reaching a peak in the 1972 basketball final. With seconds to go—and with the U.S. ahead by one point—there was great controversy over whether or not the Soviet team had called a time-out. The game was restarted several times, and right as the horn sounded for the end of the game, the Soviets scored the winning basket. The Americans shocked many people by refusing to accept the result—or their silver medals.

AGAINST THE ODDS

Winning an Olympic medal is the end of a long and often painful journey for many competitors. All Olympians have to master their own doubts and fears, push their bodies to the limit, and overcome their rivals in order to win a coveted place on the medal podium. Some competitors have, through illness, injury, or circumstance, had to go even farther than most to achieve their prize.

▲ *A year before the Sydney Olympics a motorcycle accident left French shooter Franck Dumoulin in a wheelchair. He managed not only to compete in Sydney but also to pull off an amazing display to win the 10m pistol shooting gold medal.*

▶ *Wilma Rudolph won three gold medals at the 1960 Games to add to the 4 x 100m relay bronze that she had earned as a 16 year old in 1956. Her grace and dazzling speed earned her the nickname the "Black Gazelle."*

An uphill struggle

Many competitors have battled against severe problems from childhood to become Olympic champions. Hungarian fencer Ildiko Ujlaki-Rejto was born deaf, and her training involved her coaches writing down messages for her. Despite this, she became a world-class fencer, competing in five Olympics (1960–1976) and winning seven medals. American sprinter Wilma Rudolph caught pneumonia and scarlet fever at the age of four. This left her paralyzed, with doctors saying she would never walk again. Rudolph not only learned to walk but to run—at record-breaking speed. She was the first woman to run 200m in under 23 seconds, and in 1960 she became the legend of the Rome Games by winning three gold medals in the 100m, 200m, and 4 x 100m relay.

▼ *Denmark's Lis Hartel contracted polio in her 20s, leaving her paralyzed below the knees. At both the 1952 and 1956 Games—despite having to be lifted onto and off of her horse— Hartel won silver in the equestrian dressage event.*

Amazing comebacks

Some Olympians have shown the sheer courage and determination to rebound from serious accidents or illnesses. Hungarian Oliver Halassy's case is extraordinary. He lost his left leg below the knee in a trolley accident, yet despite this he competed in the physically demanding water polo event and was part of the victorious Hungarian team at the 1936 Olympics. In 1996 American cycling legend Lance Armstrong discovered that he had potentially life-threatening testicular cancer. After a number of operations and courses of radiation treatment Armstrong battled back not only to survive the disease but also to win cycling's most coveted prize, the Tour de France, and to win a bronze medal at the Sydney Olympics.

Kip Keino

Kipchoge "Kip" Keino was a relatively unknown runner when he achieved his dream of appearing in the 1968 Mexico City Games. He was well remembered and admired afterward for an extraordinary Olympics. The Kenyan police officer was suffering from gallstones, and while in the leading group in his first event, the 10,000m, he collapsed in agony and staggered off the track with only two laps to go. He got up to his feet to complete the race, although he was later disqualified. Four days later he entered the 5,000m and won the silver medal. Still in pain, he rested in the Olympic Village on the day of the 1,500m final and then boarded a bus to the stadium. The bus became stuck in traffic, so Keino got off and jogged more than 1 mi. (2km) to the stadium. He arrived only moments before the start of the race, in which he set a fast pace in order to try to counteract the expected strong finish of the favorite, Jim Ryun of the U.S. Astonishingly, Keino kept up his speed to win gold a clear 20m ahead of Ryun.

◄ *Jim Abbott was the star pitcher of the U.S. baseball team that triumphed at the 1988 Games. Abbott was born without a right hand. When pitching, he wore a fielder's glove over his right arm, which he would transfer to his left hand right after pitching to field any balls hit back his way. Abbott later went on to have a career in professional baseball.*

◄ *Kip Keino in action at the 1972 Munich Olympics, where he won gold in the 3,000m steeplechase— despite having little experience in the event and entering the race as a challenge.*

▼ *Japanese gymnast Shun Fujimoto broke a kneecap while competing but chose to ignore the excruciating pain in order to keep his team's gold medal hopes alive. He continued, hiding his agony, telling no one, and not even using painkillers, to achieve a gold medal score.*

For the sake of the team

Every Olympian strives to do the best for his or her team. Some take this to extremes, battling through the pain barrier when many would retire. At the 1936 Games German equestrian competitor Konrad von Wangenheim fell off his horse and broke his collarbone. He continued riding and, despite suffering a second fall the following day, helped his team win the gold medal. A similar drama occurred during the 1976 Games. Japan's Shun Fujimoto was in the middle of the gymnastics floor exercises when a freak accident caused him to break his kneecap. Remarkably, he continued performing for his team. He scored 9.5 on the pommel horse before tackling the rings, where he attempted a triple somersault dismount. The landing placed enormous pressure on his injured knee, but he held his position for the judges before collapsing in pain. The 9.7 mark that Fujimoto was awarded was not only his best-ever score on that apparatus, but it was also vital in propelling the Japanese team to gold medal glory, beating the Soviet Union by only 0.4 points.

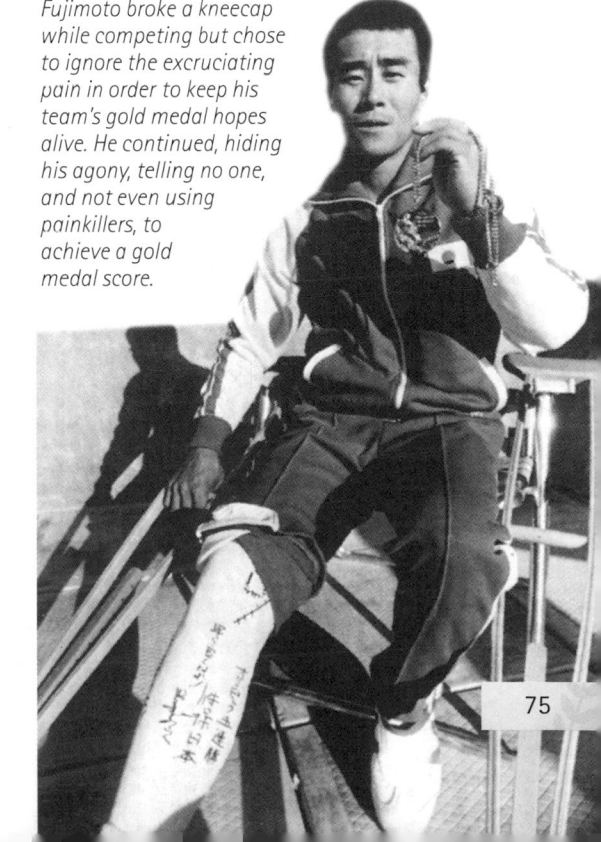

75

OLYMPIC FACTS AND FIGURES

Most career medals

Larissa Latynina, U.S.S.R., 1956–1964:
18 medals (9 gold), gymnastics
Nikolay Andrianov, U.S.S.R., 1972–1980:
15 medals (7 gold), gymnastics

Most career medals (nongymnasts)

Edoardo Mangiarotti, Italy, 1936–1960:
13 medals (6 gold), fencing
Paavo Nurmi, Finland, 1920–1928:
12 medals (9 gold), track and field
Mark Spitz, U.S., 1968–1972: 11 medals
(9 gold), swimming
Matt Biondi, U.S., 1984–1992: 11
medals (8 gold), swimming
Birgit Fischer, Germany, 1980–2000:
10 medals (7 gold), kayaking

Most medals in a single Olympics

Aleksandr Dityatin, U.S.S.R., 1980:
8 medals (3 gold), gymnastics
Mark Spitz, U.S., 1972: 7 medals
(7 gold), swimming
Willis Lee, U.S., 1920: 7 medals
(5 gold), shooting
Matt Biondi, U.S., 1988: 7 medals
(5 gold), swimming
Mariya Gorokhovskaya, U.S.S.R., 1952:
7 medals (2 gold), gymnastics

Oldest medalist

Oscar Swahn, Sweden, 1920:
aged 72 years and 280 days,
shooting silver medalist

Oldest female competitor

Lorna Johnstone, Great Britain,
1972: aged 70, placed 12th in the
dressage event

Oldest competitor in Sydney 2000

Bruce Meredith, U.S. Virgin Islands:
aged 63, shooting

Youngest competitors

Dimitrios Loundras, Greece, 1896:
aged 10, gymnastics
Carlos Front, Spain, 1992: aged 11,
coxed rowing eights
Luigina Giavotti, Italy, 1928:
aged 11, gymnastics

Games of the modern era

Year	Host city	Competitors	Nations	Events
1896	Athens, Greece	241	14	43
1900	Paris, France	1,225	24	95
1904	St. Louis, Missouri	689	13	91
1908	London, England	2,035	22	110
1912	Stockholm, Sweden	2,547	28	102
1920	Antwerp, Belgium	2,669	29	154
1924	Paris, France	3,092	44	126
1928	Amsterdam, Netherlands	3,014	46	109
1932	Los Angeles, California	1,408	37	117
1936	Berlin, Germany	4,066	49	129
1948	London, England	4,099	59	136
1952	Helsinki, Finland	4,925	69	149
1956	Melbourne, Australia	3,184	67	145
1960	Rome, Italy	5,348	83	150
1964	Tokyo, Japan	5,140	93	163
1968	Mexico City, Mexico	5,530	112	172
1972	Munich, West Germany	7,123	121	195
1976	Montreal, Canada	6,028	92	198
1980	Moscow, U.S.S.R.	5,217	80	203
1984	Los Angeles, California	6,797	140	221
1988	Seoul, South Korea	8,465	159	237
1992	Barcelona, Spain	9,367	169	257
1996	Atlanta, Georgia	10,318	197	271
2000	Sydney, Australia	10,651	199	300
2004	Athens, Greece	10,500 (approx.)	201	301
2008	Beijing, China	–	–	–

Source: International Olympic Committee web site (www.olympic.org)

STRANGE BUT TRUE

In 1900 American Margaret Abbot entered what she thought was just a local golf competition. When she won, she became the first women's Olympic champion of the event.

Yachtsman Hank Lammens was disqualified from the 1992 Games for forgetting his life jacket.

Australian Henry Pearce was so dominant in the 1928 single sculls rowing event that he stopped to let a group of ducks pass before continuing his rowing to win gold.

South African boxer Thomas Hamilton-Brown lost a close bout at the 1936 Games and consoled himself with a hearty meal. When officials discovered that Hamilton-Brown had actually won, he was too heavy to compete in the next round.

Cuban runner Felix Carbajal turned up for the 1904 marathon in heavy shoes and long pants, having hitchhiked many miles. During the race Carbajal became hungry and ate some green apples from a tree. A stomachache forced him to withdraw from the race.

During the 1932 discus event Frenchman Jules Noël drank champagne between throws. He lost out on a bronze medal by 10cm.

American athlete George Eyser won the rope climbing, parallel bars, and vault gymnastics events in the 1904 Olympics despite having a wooden leg.

Officials at the 1932 Games lost count of the laps in the 3,000m steeplechase and forced the athletes to run a 3,400m-long race as a result.

Two of the boats competing in the 1900 sailing competition were disqualified for using secret motors.

A 100m freestyle race for sailors was held in 1896, with entrance restricted to members of the Greek navy.

Neither Giovanni Pettenella nor Pierre Trentin wanted to make the first move in their 1,000m cycling semifinal in 1964. They stood still on their pedals for 21 minutes and 57 seconds. Pettenella went on to win the race and the eventual gold medal.

The cycling course at the 1920 Games included a grade railroad crossing. Some cyclists were delayed by more than four minutes while waiting for a train to pass.

When Canadian George Lyon won the 1904 golf competition, he walked on his hands up to the stage to receive the trophy.

The combined Danish and Swedish tug-of-war team in the 1900 Games was one man short, so a Danish journalist, Edgar Aaybe, was asked to join in. He went on to win a gold medal.

MEMORABLE MOMENTS

The Summer Olympics have generated hundreds of memorable moments of triumph, disaster, courage, and friendship. Many of these moments are contained in the rest of this book. Here are a further five.

Stopwatch sportsmanship
Finland's Paavo Nurmi had already won eight Olympic gold medals in long- and middle-distance running events when he lined up for the semifinal of the 3,000m steeplechase at the 1928 Games. Famous for running with a stopwatch in his hand, Nurmi fell and dropped the watch in the water jump. French athlete Lucien Duquesne stopped to help him recover the watch. Nurmi responded by running alongside Duquesne and offering him first place at the finish line, but the Frenchman declined.

The ultimate athlete
Mildred "Babe" Didrikson was an incredible all-around athlete who excelled in baseball, basketball, and, after her Olympic career, golf, which she played professionally. At the age of 21 Didrikson qualified for eight Olympic events at the 1932 Games but was only allowed to compete in three. She won the javelin with an Olympic record and then the 80m hurdles in a world-record time of 11.7 seconds. In the high jump Didrikson and her American teammate Jean Shiley recorded the same height, but Didrikson was demoted to a silver medal for her unusual jumping technique. Didrikson is considered to be one of the greatest female athletes of all time.

The barefoot wonder
Ethiopian long-distance runner Abebe Bikila arrived for the 1960 marathon as a virtual unknown. He was also very inexperienced, having only ever run two marathons before. Bikila triumphed to great acclaim, winning the gold medal and breaking the world record with a time of two hours, 15 minutes, and 16 seconds. He achieved this by running in bare feet, even though part of the course was made up of cobblestoned streets. Bikila wowed Olympic spectators four years later by winning the marathon again, this time only six weeks after an appendix operation.

Five in a row
In 1996 Great Britain's Steve Redgrave set an Olympic rowing record by becoming the first person to win gold medals at four consecutive Games in this punishing sport. Redgrave trained relentlessly for Sydney 2000, despite suffering periodically from colitis—an inflammation of the large intestine—and having been diagnosed as a diabetic at the age of 35. In a tight final in the coxless fours event, with their Italian rivals edging even closer, Redgrave and his rowing partners held on to secure Redgrave's fifth gold in as many Olympics. No one in any endurance sport had ever achieved such a feat before.

The "Super Eagles" arrive
At the Atlanta Games of 1996 the Nigerian soccer team, nicknamed the "Super Eagles," starred in one of the most exciting games in Olympic history. Losing 3–1 to favorites Brazil in the semifinal, the Super Eagles responded with two late goals to take the game into extra time. They scored again to claim an astonishing 4–3 victory against the world champions and went on to beat Argentina in the final—becoming the first African nation to win soccer gold.

GLOSSARY

Amateur A person who plays a sport without being paid for it. Early Olympics were open only to amateur athletes, but today both amateurs and **professionals** take part.

Anabolic steroids Drugs that encourage muscle growth and allow an athlete to become stronger. They are banned in Olympic sports.

Apartheid A political system that kept apart the white and non-white people of South Africa. It was dismantled in the 1990s.

Artistic merit In sports such as gymnastics the originality, smoothness, and grace of a competitor's routine.

Baton A short bar carried by one runner for each leg of a track-and-field **relay** race.

Bout A contest or fight in a sport such as boxing, wrestling, or judo.

Boycott A refusal to attend an event, such as the Olympics, often for political reasons.

Choreographed Carefully planned out in advance.

Cold War A period of political hostility between the U.S. and the Soviet Union after World War II. It ended with the breakup of the Soviet Union in the early 1990s.

Dehydration Loss of water. Athletes may suffer from dehydration during very hot conditions.

Demonstration sport A sport performed at the Olympics without medals being offered.

Discontinued sport A sport that has been dropped from the Olympic program such as tug-of-war.

Disqualification The exclusion of an athlete from a race or, if it has already been run, the removal of an athlete's place and time from the race records.

Doping The illegal use of a substance that can improve an athlete's performance and that may be harmful to the athlete's health.

Dribble To propel a ball while running by repeatedly tapping it with the hand, the foot, or a stick in sports such as basketball, soccer, and field hockey.

Endurance sport A sport in which competitors must perform for a long time such as rowing or a marathon.

Execute To perform (a move) in a sport such as gymnastics or diving.

Extra time An additional period played at the end of a game if the two teams have tied.

False start The beginning of a race in which a competitor leaves the **starting blocks** before the starter's pistol is fired. The race must be restarted.

Fatigue Tiredness caused by the effort of doing an activity.

Flag bearer An athlete who carries the flag of his or her national team at the opening ceremony of the Olympics.

Fosbury flop A high jumping technique where the jumper clears the bar headfirst and backward. It is named after American athlete Dick Fosbury, who perfected the jump.

Freestyle In swimming freestyle means that swimmers can choose to race using any stroke, although in practice the front crawl is always used. In sports such as synchronized swimming and equestrian dressage freestyle means that the competitors perform their own routines rather than a set series of moves.

Hamstring A tendon (length of tissue) that attaches a muscle to the back of the knee.

Heat A qualification race in the early stages of a competition.

Homestretch In track and field the last 100m of a race.

Host nation The country that stages an event such as the Olympics.

IOC Short for International Olympic Committee—the organization that governs and runs the Summer and Winter Olympic Games.

Kick A burst of speed, often toward the end of a race.

Marshal A person who helps organize an event.

Merchandise Items for sale at an event such as souvenirs, clothing, and toys.

Modern era In Olympic terms the period from the first modern Games in 1896 to the present day.

Olympian A competitor in the Olympic Games.

Olympic flame The fire that burns in a cauldron in the main stadium throughout an Olympic Games.

Olympic movement All the individuals and organizations that help stage and promote the Olympic Games.

Olympic rings The key symbol of the Olympic Games, formed of five interlocking rings that represent the continents that take part: Africa, the Americas, Asia, Australasia, and Europe.

Olympic torch The torch used to carry the **Olympic flame** from Greece to the host city before the start of each Olympics.

Paralympian A competitor in the Paralympic games for athletes with disabilities or special needs.

Penalty shoot-out A way of deciding the outcome of a game of soccer when the scores are tied after **extra time**.

Photo finish A very close finish of a race. The judges examine a special photograph, triggered electronically, to determine the medal placement.

Podium A raised platform that competitors stand on to receive a medal.

Professional A person who receives money for playing a sport. See also **amateur**.

Relay A race between two or more teams in which each competitor in the team covers part of the total distance, known as a leg.

Sponsorship Money from private companies that is used to promote sports or athletes.

Springboard A flexible board used to gain height or speed in diving or artistic gymnastics.

Stamina The ability to keep performing at close to maximum effort over long periods of time.

Starting blocks Devices used by sprinters and swimmers at the start of a race. Set at an angle, they support the feet and help the competitor gain speed quickly.

Stopboard A raised board at the end of a javelin runway or at the front of a discus or hammer circle. A throw made by an athlete whose foot crosses the stopboard is not legal.

Technical merit The level of difficulty of a competitor's routine in sports such as gymnastics and synchronized swimming.

Time-out An interruption in play during a game, such as basketball, in which players rest or discuss tactics or when substitutions are made.

Velodrome An arena with a sloped track for cycling races.

Warning paddle A colored bat held up by an official to warn a racewalker that he or she has broken the rules.

WEB SITES

www.olympic.org
The home page of the International Olympic Committee (IOC). This substantial web site contains details about all the previous Olympics, famous Olympians, and the many events featured in the Summer and Winter Games.

www.athens2004.gr
The official web site of the 2004 Summer Games held in Athens, Greece, with pages in English. News, details of events, and features on the venues and preparations behind the Games are all displayed.

http://en.beijing-2008.org/
The official web site of the 2008 Summer games, which will be held in China's capital city, Beijing.

www.paralympic.org/
The web site of the International Paralympic Committee, containing information on the Paralympics, and results from the Games.

www.specialolympics.org/
The web site of the Special Olympics movement, which assists over one million people with special needs in their quest to play sports.

www.iaaf.org
The official site of The International Association of Athletics Federations. This body manages track-and-field events worldwide. Its web site is the place to go for details of athletes' rankings and current world records in track-and-field events.

www.clivegifford.co.uk/ inprint/Olympics.htm
A collection of pages on the Olympics from the author of this book, with quizzes, updated news, highlights, and trivia from the Summer Games.

www.wada-ama.org
The internet home of the World Anti-Doping Agency (WADA) contains news on the fight against drugs in sports, lists banned and prohibited substances, and details the latest testing initiatives.

www.perseus.tufts.edu/ Olympics
Using material taken from an extensive museum collection on the ancient Greeks, this web site provides a detailed and fascinating look at the ancient Olympics.

www.olympic-usa.org/
The web pages of the United States Olympic Committee, this site is full of news about competitions and athletes, as well as interesting information on many of the events that feature in the Olympics.

INDEX

Abbott, Jim 75
Ainslie, Ben 47
Ajose, Olusegun 53
Ajunwa, Chioma 30
Alfararjeh, Mohammad 9
Amsterdam 1928 8, 9, 23, 76, 77
ancient Olympics 6, 7, 10, 37
Andrianov, Nikolay 76
Antwerp 1920 8, 9, 46, 76, 77
archery 49, 50
Armstrong, Lance 71, 74
Arzhannikova, Ljudmila 50
Athens 1896 5, 6, 8, 27, 31, 42, 76
Athens 2004 5, 6, 13, 17, 46, 76
Atlanta 1996 9, 17, 64, 66, 76, 77
Attolico, Francesco 45

badminton 59, 68
Bagger, Marie 33
Balas, Iolanda 32
Barcelona 1992 9, 13, 58–59, 76
baseball 59, 64, 75, 77
Basilio de Sotelo, Enriqueta 40
basketball 20, 21, 58, 59, 64, 65, 73, 77
beach volleyball 66, 67
Beamon, Bob 41
Beijing 2008 12, 76
Benoit, Joan 27
Beresh, Oleksandr 57
Berlin 1936 7, 20–21, 46, 48, 66, 76
Bikila, Abebe 77
Biondi, Matt 49, 76
Bird, Larry 58
Blankers-Koen, Fanny 22
boxing 6, 11, 18, 52, 53, 73, 76
boycotts 5, 40, 48, 58, 73
Braye, Stuart 7
Brits, Okkert 33
Bubka, Sergei 33, 59
Budd, Zola 24
Byun Jong-Il 18

canoe/kayak 20, 46, 47, 76
Carlos, John 40
Caslavska, Vera 40, 41
Charkova, Olga 51
Christie, Linford 17, 18, 48, 59
Clay, Cassius 53
closing ceremonies 5, 71
Comaneci, Nadia 57
Cook, Natalie 67
Cook, Stephanie 39
cycling 10, 19, 39, 41, 49, 60–61, 74, 77

de Bruijn, Inge 42, 43, 71
de Coubertin, Baron Pierre 5, 6, 7
decathlon 11, 38, 39, 72
Decker, Mary 24
Devers, Gail 22, 29
di Donna, Roberto 51
Didrikson, Mildred "Babe" 77
discontinued sports 8, 9, 20
discus 8, 36–37, 39, 77
disqualifications 17, 18, 27, 41, 48, 72, 75, 77
diving 21, 44, 49, 71
Douillet, David 54
dressage 63, 74, 76
drugs 9, 19, 41, 48
Dumoulin, Franck 74
Duquesne, Lucien 77

Ebnoutalib, Faissal 9
Edwards, Jonathan 31
Emerick, Viviani 67
Erychov, Alexander 45
eventing 63
Ezzine, Ali 29

Fairbrother, Nicola 54
fencing 18, 21, 39, 49, 50, 51, 74, 76
Ferrazzi, Pierpaolo 47
field hockey 18, 58, 59, 64, 65, 73
Fischer, Birgit 71, 76
flag 5, 7
Flagothier, Nicole 54
flame 5, 7, 40
Fosbury, Dick 32, 40
Fraser, Dawn 43
Freeman, Cathy 70
Fujimoto, Shun 75

Garcia, Anier 17
Gebrselassie, Haile 26, 72, 73
Gestring, Marjorie 21
Ghaffari, Siamak 52
Goldstein, Margie 62
golf 8, 9, 76, 77
Graf, Steffi 49
Gray, Tanni 58
Greene, Maurice 14, 23
gymnastics 20, 41, 56–57, 59, 75, 76, 77

Halassy, Oliver 21, 74
Hamilton, Suzy Favor 16
hammer throw 34–35
handball 20, 66, 67
Harju, Arsi 35
Hartel, Lis 74
Helsinki 1952 26, 38, 76
Hemery, David 41
heptathlon 38, 39, 49
high jump 8, 11, 32–33, 38, 39, 40, 77
Hingsen, Jürgen 72
hosting the Olympics 12–13, 16–17
Hoy, Andrew 63
hurdles 17, 28–29, 38, 39, 40, 41, 77
Hylton, Mark 29

International Olympic Committee (IOC) 5, 6, 9, 12, 19, 41
Ivanov, Vyacheslav 47

javelin 6, 36, 37, 39, 77
Jensen, Knut 19, 41
Johnson, Ben 48
Johnson, Magic 58
Johnson, Michael 14, 24
Jordan, Michael 58
Joyner-Kersee, Jackie 38, 49
Juantorena, Alberto 24, 25
judo 54–55, 59
jumping (equestrian) 39, 62

Kafelnikov, Yevgeny 69
Kail, Darren 55
Karavaeva, Irina 56
Karelin, Aleksandr 52, 71
Karjalainen, Olli-Pekka 34
Karolchik, Yanina 35
kayaking see canoe/kayak
Keino, Kipchoge "Kip" 75
Kenteris, Konstantinos 23
Kolehmainen, Hannes 10
Kondylis, Konstantin 20
Korbut, Olga 56, 57
Korzeniowski, Robert 27
Kosgei, Reuben 29

Ladejo, Du'aine 29
Latynina, Larissa 76
Law, Leslie 63
Lewis, Carl 23, 30, 48
Lewis, Denise 39
London 1908 8, 13, 27, 42, 76
London 1948 7, 23, 76
Long, Luz 21
long jump 6, 21, 30–31, 38, 39, 41, 49
Longo-Ciprelli, Jeannie 61
Los Angeles 1932 8, 76, 77
Los Angeles 1984 5, 24, 27, 38, 45, 76
Louganis, Greg 49
Louis, Spiridon 6
Lyons, Paul 55

Mangiarotti, Edoardo 76
marathons 6, 18, 26, 27, 41, 48, 76, 77
Marcz, Tamas 45
Martinez, Miguel 60
Mathias, Bob 38
McMahon, Brigitte 39
medals 7, 11, 76, 77
Melbourne 1956 18, 62, 66, 70
Mexico City 1968 9, 18, 19, 40–41, 75
Meyer, Elana 59
middle-distance running 24–25
Miller, Scott 42
Minchev, Sevdalin 19
Montreal 1976 5, 18, 57, 76
Moscow 1980 5, 76
Moses, Edwin 28
mountain biking 9, 60
Munich 1972 18, 19, 43, 66, 73, 76
Mutola, Maria 24

Na Li 44
Nummerdor, Reinder 67
Nurmi, Paavo 76, 77

Oatley-Nist, Kristy 63
O'Connor, David 63
Oerter, Al 36, 40
Olympic Village 13, 17
Onischenko, Boris 18
opening ceremonies 4, 5, 7, 10, 15, 20, 40, 48, 58
Owens, Jesse 21

Palfi, Judit 51
Palios, Edgardo 65
Papp, Laszlo 53
Paralympics 7, 51, 55, 58, 65
Paris 1900 6, 8, 9, 34, 46, 66, 76, 77
Paris 1924 9, 76
Pascual, Rafael 67
pentathlon, modern 10, 11, 39
Pérec, Marie-José 23
Perkins, Kieren 43
Pinsent, Matthew 46
Pippen, Scottie 58
Polasik, Jadwiga 51
pole vault 32, 33, 39, 71
Popov, Alexsandr 42
Pottharst, Kerri 67
Price-Smith, Connie 35

racewalking 26, 27, 41
Radcliffe, Paula 14
Raskina, Yulia 56
Redgrave, Steve 46, 70, 71, 77
Redmond, Derek 59
rivalries 72–73
Rogge, Jacques 12
Rolton, Gillian 63
Rome 1960 19, 53, 74, 76

Rose, Ralph 11
rowing 46, 47, 59, 70, 71, 76, 77
Rudolph, Wilma 74

Sabatini, Gabriela 49
sailing 46, 47, 59, 76, 77
Samaranch, Juan Antonio 61
Scherbo, Vitaly 59
Seoul 1988 18, 30, 38, 48–49, 76
Shanmuganathan, Kuhan 65
Shinohara, Shinichi 54
shooting 39, 50, 51, 74, 76
shot put 11, 34, 35, 38, 39, 49
Skolimowska, Kamila 34
Small, Kristina 65
Smith, Tommie 40
soccer 66, 77
softball 64
Sohn Kee-chung 48
Spitz, Mark 43, 76
sprints 14, 17, 21, 22–23, 38, 39, 48, 74
St. Louis 1904 8, 18, 44, 76, 77
steeplechase 29, 41, 75, 77
Stockholm 1912 5, 10–11, 44, 76
Stratton, Sarah 71
Suleymanoglu, Naim 52
swimming 42–3
Sydney 2000 5, 7, 9, 13, 16, 17, 19, 27, 31, 39, 46–47, 52, 56, 70–71, 73, 76
Sydorenko, Sergiy 55
symbols 7, 58, 70
synchronized swimming 44, 45
Szabo, Gabriela 25

table tennis 49, 68–69
tae kwon do 9, 54, 55, 71
tennis 49, 68, 69
Tergat, Paul 72, 73
Thompson, Daley 38, 72
Thorpe, Ian 43, 71
Thorpe, Jim 11
Tichy, Peter 26
Todd, Mark 63
Tokyo 1964 66, 76, 77
trampolining 56
triathlon 39, 71
triple jump 30, 31
tug-of-war 8, 77
Tulu, Derartu 59

Ujlaki-Rejto, Ildiko 74

volleyball 66, 67, 71, 73
von Wangenheim, Konrad 75

water polo 16, 18, 21, 45, 74
weight lifting 8, 52, 71, 73
Williams, Venus 69
Williams Junior, Ricardo 53
Wilson, Blaine 57
Winkler, Hans-Günter 62
Winter Olympics 5, 7, 49
wrestling 6, 10, 11, 52
Wyludda, Ilke 36

Xue Sang 44

Yelesina, Yelena 32
Yoo Yong-Sung 68
Young, Ernie 64

Zamolodtchikova, Elena 57
Zatopek, Emil 26
Zelezny, Jan 37
Zijlaard, Leontien 61
Zimmerman, Iris 51